BOOKS ALIVE!

BOOKS ALIVE!

Using Literature
in the Classroom

Susan Hill

PEGUIS
PUBLISHERS

Winnipeg Manitoba Canada

Printed and bound in Canada by Hignell Printing Limited ✪

94 95 96 97 98 5 4 3 2 1

Canadian Cataloguing in Publication Data

Hill, Susan

    Books alive!

    Originally published: Melbourne: T. Nelson
Australia, 1986.
    Includes bibliographical references and index.
    ISBN 1-895411-71-8

    1. Literature – Study and teaching (Elementary) 2. Reading (Elementary)
    3. Children – Books and reading. I. Title.

LB1575.H48 1994   372.64   C94-920201-0

Book Design and Art Direction: Laura Ayers
Cover Illustration and Design: Craig Terlson
Illustrations: Juli Kent

Grateful acknowledgment is made to the following for use of copyright material: Random House for the illustration by Shirley Hughes (page 80) from *Cinderella or the Little Glass Slipper* by Charles Perrault; Faber & Faber for the illustration by Errol Le Cain (page 80) from *Cinderella or the Little Glass Slipper* by Charles Perrault; Heinemann for the illustration by Arthur Rackham (page 80) from *Cinderella* retold by C. S. Evans; HarperCollins for the illustration and text (page 54) from *Outside Over There* by Maurice Sendak; Scholastic for the illustration and text from *Over in the Meadow* illustrated by Ezra Jack Keats (page 54).

The publishers also wish to thank Yolanda Hogeveen for her contribution to chapter 4, "The Author and Illustrator," as well as the librarians of the Children's Department, Winnipeg Public Library.

Peguis Publishers Limited
100–318 McDermot Avenue
Winnipeg, Manitoba
Canada R3A 0A2

CONTENTS

PREFACE

Watching a group of children poring over an open book as they share a familiar text or suddenly coming across a reader buried in a book in a quiet corner represents to me the essential elements of a literature-based reading program. Literature is to be shared by a community of readers where responses are generated and extended through interaction with others; it is also a quiet reflective pleasure, experiencing another world created collaboratively by the author and the reader. The rich content of literature provides the ideas that stimulate response, whether it be a group response in the form of a discussion, a mural, a play, or the individual response of a giggle or a tear.

Orchestrating a literature-based reading program takes a light hand; overplanning can well lead to repetitive, dull, and monotonous book reports. A light touch allows the teacher to observe and follow the leads of children as they create meaning in the stories they read.

One way for a teacher to follow the leads of children is to have ideas ready to stimulate, critique, and extend the interaction between readers and books. To do this, a teacher may organize literature-based reading programs around the following approaches:

➡ response
➡ author
➡ story
➡ great books

These approaches may become the focus of the reading program at different times. Sometimes children may respond to stories in the form of art, drama, poetry, or quiet reflection. At other times a reader may decide to concentrate on a particular author and read all the books in a particular series. Readers and reader-writers may want to find out more about the various elements found in stories, and here the story will be the focus. In some classes the great books—the classics—will be read aloud or shared in small literature groups for a while.

This book presents ideas for literature-based reading programs and contains many suggestions for teachers in following up the leads given by readers. These ideas enable the teacher to follow children's responses and provide support for them in their particular quests for meaning while reading real books.

I am indebted to Joelie Hancock for her comments on this book and to Karen Cornelius, Beverley Endersbee, Sue Le Busque, Meredith Kennedy, Anna Kalionas, Jackie Miers, Rita Purvis, Trish Widera, and Helen Kerin and their students for ideas on literature-based reading. Virginia Lee, Linda Blackstone, and Beth Ganser typed the manuscript and many of the photographs were taken by Ray Stradwick. Judy Bunney, Sherrie Rutter, and the library staff at the University of South Australia helped with the references.

Susan Hill
University of South Australia

WHY LITERATURE-BASED READING?

Using real books as the content of a reading program provides a rich variety of experiences. Children may read fantasy tales, realistic stories, or myths and legends. By reading real books, the notion of reading for enjoyment is fostered, and as children learn to select books from the immense range available, they also learn that there is a book for every purpose: books to escape into, books to learn from, books that present new ideas, and books to just sit back and enjoy. Selecting and reading real books provide readers of all ages with the opportunity to practice reading while immersed in a story that is rich and rewarding in itself.

Literature can be defined as writing which is concerned with exploring the value and meaning of human experience by imaginative recreation in language. It is writing that is highly valued by an individual or by a group of people. It may include stories and poems written by children in the classroom, which are often very important to the class and the teacher. Literature, if we use this definition, is subject to society's views and the views of individuals. At particular times in history certain kinds of writing were highly regarded but lost favor later. For example, the writing of several centuries ago is less highly valued today. What it is that constitutes literature then may range from the literary award-winning book of the year to the classroom-published stories of primary school children.

Literature has greater value than just providing the content of a reading program. It helps the reader better understand worlds perhaps not yet experienced, extends the imagination and helps us deal better with life's problems. Literature also provides a base for developing all aspects of the language arts: talking, listening, reading, and writing.

Literature and understanding the world

Children's literature presents an enormously wide range of situations, characters, plots, themes, and writing styles. However, more than merely presenting an interesting variety of ideas, literature may play a central role in how humans come to structure and understand their world. Barbara Hardy (1968) from the University of London suggests that all human beings' constructions of reality are, in fact, stories that we tell ourselves about how the world works.

She suggests

> We dream in narrative, day-dream in narrative, remember, anticipate, hope, despair, believe, doubt, plan, revise, criticize, construct, gossip, learn, hate, love by narrative

Young children, for example, continually act out stories to help explain, interpret, and understand their emotions. A young child sent to his room will tell stories about how mean and unkind his parents are and how he plans to run away. This is the story of Maurice Sendak's *Where the Wild Things Are* and perhaps this retelling of a familiar story—a child banished to the bedroom, a fantasy runaway adventure and the return home to a kind, accepting family—explains, in part, why this book is so very popular with young children.

Literature and the imagination

Literature will indeed help children vicariously experience life, but it is also concerned with developing the imagination and emotions. Miller (1979) claims that good children's literature can educate the heart as well as the head:

> Through literature we are enabled to know what it means to be someone else, to know what it is to think another's thoughts, to feel another's emotions, to live another's life. Through the imagination we are liberated from the confinements of our own brief time and our own small space. And we are released from the bonds of our local visions, from the narrowness of our own parochial values.

Through literature children extend their experiences and the boundaries of their vision. Chukovsky (1963), the Russian poet, tells us that a child's understanding is enhanced through good stories that

> consist of fostering in the child, at whatever cost, compassion and humanness...this miraculous ability to be disturbed by another being's misfortunes, to feel joy about another being's happiness, to experience another's fate as our own.

Children's literature can help to develop compassion for others, stimulate and develop the imagination and, as suggested by Bruno Bettelheim (1977) in *The Uses of Enchantment*, some children's literature plays a large role in developing a child's moral values.

Literature and language development

The effects of storytelling and reading aloud to young children have been studied by many linguists and educational researchers. Carol Chomsky (1973) found a high correlation between a child's linguistic stages of development and previous exposure to literature. Eileen M. Burke (1979) similarly found that exposure to a vast range of literature, with well-developed characters, plots, settings, and use of alliteration, onomatopoeia, rhyme, rhythm, and unusual syntactical patterns and twists, provides opportunities for the child to think about and reflect on language. Children's literature can present unusual situations, characters, and events, often using symbolism and figurative language. The use of symbolism and figurative language—such as "kick the bucket," "he was a bear of a man," "this is a prison," "faster than a speeding bullet," for example—is a way to describe and construct the reality of the world. Many basal reading schemes do not use figurative language that evokes human emotion and ideas and may come across as somewhat bland.

Literature and reading development

Familiarity with the language of books allows readers to set up expectations of language they may meet in stories. Understanding book language begins with hearing stories read aloud and grows as readers encounter more and more books encompassing a range of literary styles. Margaret Meek (1984) points out that book language also incorporates intertext references to other books. For example, the book *Clever Polly and the Stupid Wolf*, by Catherine Storr, is most successful when readers relate it to another familiar story, *Little Red Riding Hood*. Often books make reference to other books, stories, authors, and events, and knowledge of a range of stories is essential for future reading development.

Reading a range of literature enables children to switch pace as well as change expectations about how a story is to unfold. Reading a book by Enid Blyton calls for quick skimming of the surface text and easy matching of the surface structure with the deep structure of the fast-moving plot. Other books demand more care in reading. *The Iron Man* by Ted Hughes calls for careful reading as the complex sentence structure in the early pages forces the reader to pause in order to grasp the meaning. Often the books that demand more of the reader are those remembered as "a great book to read."

Literature and writing development

Stories told and read by children act as models or structures for them to make their own stories. Each new story made up by a child is a product of his or her ideas and past experiences generated through books, real life experiences, reflections, and transformations. When discussing children's storytelling, Mikkelsen (1984) says:

> Whether children are talking or telling, their storymaking involves a process of making sense of stories, of discovering with each new narrative exploration a different piece of the story puzzle that sends all the coloured crystals slipping into a new configuration, forming a new story pattern which enlarges and expands the one told or read or talked about before. Children blend, recreate, borrow, and transform various story elements in their writing.

While literature indirectly influences a child's writing, writing about literature experiences allows the reader to get inside both the reading and writing processes to understand how good writing really works. Some teachers (Nancie Atwell 1984) invite children to write down their ideas about books, authors, meanings, ideas, likes, and dislikes. When children do this, Atwell claims that knowledge about being an author is transferred to the student's own written stories, not only in the use of plot ideas, but also in the variation of style and descriptive language, imagery, and sentence construction.

Literature and bibliotherapy

Bibliotherapy is an interesting technique that can be used as children vicariously experience situations that help them to solve some of their own emotional problems. For example, a child whose parents are in the process of being divorced may understand the situation a little better after reading a book such as *My Dad Lives in a Downtown Hotel* by Peggy Mann. Cultural awareness may develop with reading biographies, historical fiction, fantasy, and adventure stories set in other cultures.

No one doubts that literature is important for providing children with good reading material but it is also an ideal method for children to learn about themselves, others, and the world. It is a major influence on children's personal growth and their language and writing development. It also has a major influence on their attitudes to and performance in reading development. Ways of using literature in the classroom are diverse and center around interacting with different kinds of books and the interests of different kinds of readers.

APPROACHES TO TEACHING LITERATURE

Ways of exploring literature and theories about literature have changed over time. Centuries ago it was thought important to read and discuss the great books, books that presented worthwhile social values, or books that had stood the test of time such as *Pilgrim's Progress*. In the nineteenth century, there was a preoccupation with finding out more about the author and how he or she came to write particular books. In the early twentieth century, the New Criticism was concerned with exploring elements within a text or story. Recently there has been a marked shift of attention to the reader and his or her response to a text (Reception Theory, Eagleton 1983).

The process of reading according to reception theory is a complex and dynamic one. The reader brings to the work certain understandings and as reading proceeds, these understandings will be modified by what is read. Several children reading a story may respond quite differently to it as Galda (1983) demonstrates when discussing books with primary school children. Discussing responses to stories in a group may influence the group's interpretation as individual responses are modified and extended. When focusing on the response to a story, the reader's creation of the story and personal interpretation are paramount.

While reader response is a favored approach and is to be encouraged within every interaction between a child and a story, it is appropriate at times to use other means to explore literature. It is important to find out about children's book authors and illustrators in order to appreciate fully a work of literature. It is also important to explore how stories work, to find out why characterization, plot, and theme are essential elements. Similarly, it is important to find out about the great books, classics that have continued to be read.

A literature-based reading program may concentrate on each of these areas at various times:

- the response
- the author
- the story
- the great books

By focusing on one or a combination of these areas, teachers and children can develop a variety of ways of working with literature-based reading programs in the classroom.

The response

With this approach, the reader's response to the text is the essential element. Sometimes it will be a sigh or a yawn, but at other times poetry, songs, dramatic presentations, stories, and books are produced as responses by children. When responding to literature, the reader interacts with a book in such a way that the book comes alive in his or her mind by the personal experiences, ideas, and thoughts that are brought to the text. Each reader, with different experiences and thoughts may, in fact, create a new story in his or her mind. Teachers taking this approach must foster, encourage, and extend these personal responses.

The author

When focusing on authors or author-illustrators, children will learn about the various techniques and styles they use. Sometimes children may wish to read all the books written in a particular series or all the books written by a particular author, for example, books by Lois Lowry, Betsy Byars, or Jon Scieszka. Sometimes, children will write to authors to find out more about them or to express their ideas or responses to the books they have read. This approach explores what it is to be an author, what makes an author write, and examines different children's book authors and illustrators.

The story

By concentrating on the story, children will learn about various literary genres, for example, adventure, science fiction, comedy, historical fiction. Factors that make up a story, such as setting, characters, plot, and action, may be discussed. Just what comprises a good story, literary technique, literary symbols, and essential components of any story may be explored.

The great books

Sometimes, tried and tested favorites such as *The Wizard of Oz* or fairytales such as *Snow White* will make up the literature program. When a program focuses on the great books, the content will comprise old favorites from myths and legends, fairytales and classic tales. Many teachers believe it is important for children to experience books such as these as they are often an important part of their cultural heritage.

In any one literature program, a teacher may cover one of these approaches for a week, a month, or longer. Many teachers, however, combine aspects of all these areas, thereby encouraging children to learn more about authors, find out about stories, read the classics or great books and, of course, talk, write, create, and share their responses to literature.

RESPONDING TO LITERATURE ③

Experiencing literature or being engaged with a story in its fullest sense involves a transaction or collaboration between the reader and the text. Readers actually bring their own experiences to a story. In fact, many literary theorists claim that each reader creates a new story because there is such a range of different experiences (Rosenblatt 1978). At times, a reader immersed in a book will sit back and say, "Ah ha!" as the story comes alive. At other times a story may prompt a reader to reach out to another person and to express some thoughts about it.

As new stories are created in the minds of readers, a teacher of literature has an important role in encouraging response to literature. At times the response may simply be a sigh or a frown, but at other times students may talk, argue, debate, dramatize, paint, or write about their experiences with books. Encouraging response to literature is a delicate teaching art. Dull, repetitious questioning will quell a student's enjoyment and blunt and deaden the story as it is held in the reader's mind. Repetitious book reports, either spoken or written, will extinguish the magic and glow of any good story.

Careful, perceptive discussion by a teacher may, however, extend children's responses to a book by calling to mind some key events or ideas. Often discussion of these ideas serves to enhance the literature experience. An open-ended question such as

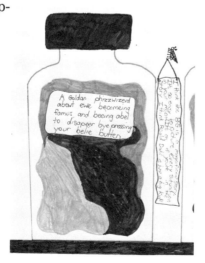

"What did this book make you think about?" may generate a range of responses from a group of children. Such open questions encourage individual responses, call for reflection by the reader, and safeguard against the fear of being wrong in responding to a teacher's questions. As with all teachers' questions, the less the teacher says the better. Of course, there are many times when there is no need to ask questions at all as the response may be personal and silent.

Asking questions about literature

There are many different levels of questioning that encourage various responses. Questions can be classified as broad or narrow, open or closed. Some questions demand simple memory recall, whereas others demand synthesis and evaluation.

Charlotte Huck developed this way of generating questions about books (see figure) based on the work of Benjamin Bloom (1956). It is generally agreed that the first question asked should lead a child back to the book. For example, taking the story *Aranea* by Jenny Wagner and Ron Brooks, a teacher may ask narrow memory questions that invite a child to recall the story. Further questions may encourage interpretation, then the child may be asked to evaluate the story. Some sample questions could be:

Evaluation based on various criteria

Synthesis creating a new form

Analysis How, why, compare

Application How can you?

Interpretation How, why?

Translation Same thing written in another form

Memory What, where, when, who

NARROW – CLOSED / BROAD – OPEN

Questioning in literature (Huck, 1976)

- ▸ Memory (closed)
  - Where did Aranea make her web?
  - Where did Aranea go when it rained?

- ▸ Children's interpretation (open)
  - How do you think Aranea felt in the storm?
  - Do you think Aranea chose to live near the house? Why?

- ▸ Children's evaluation (closed or open)
  - Do the black and white illustrations suit the book? Why?
  - Does this story seem true to you? Why?

All in all, the key to discussing books with children is to watch for their responses and then follow their leads.

Oral response

Often children have difficulty in describing their ideas about a book, especially if they have had little previous experience with book discussion. To help these children, teachers should spend time talking about their own feelings about books using terminology such as *illustrations, character, language, involvement, imagination, thrill, shiver, wonder, excitement, suspense, fear, horror,* and as many other words as possible to describe their engagement with and response to a book. After some teacher-led discussions, children soon get the idea that describing thoughts, ideas, and top-of-the-head flights of fancy are fine in a book discussion. It is important to remember that at times it may be impossible to verbalize just what a book has meant to a reader. Some books need several readings and in some cases the response changes each time the book is read.

Book discussions may be child-teacher book conferences or peer-peer conferences; group conferences or whole class discussion. With a group conference it is useful if all children in the group have read the same book or had the book read to them so that ideas can be shared, extended, argued, and debated. Long, tedious book discussions are best avoided in favor of the spontaneous oral response that occurs in a trusting environment. At times, of course, the best thing to do after reading a book that has made an impact on the reader is to go on quickly and read another book.

Ways to encourage oral response

PANEL DISCUSSION

Organize a panel discussion with several children who have read the same book. Children will probably have different opinions about

➡ their favorite character
➡ the most absorbing page
➡ the part they would like to change
➡ the dullest part of the book
➡ the part where the author writes best of all

ADVERTISEMENTS

Verbally advertise the book children like best of all. Advertisements could be made on tape for radio, on video for television, or on paper for a newspaper. Discuss ways to capture the audience's attention, words to use, colors to use or sound effects.

PUPPETS

Puppets can be made from a range of materials. Make puppet plays as a way of encouraging response to books. Moving the puppets and combining puppet action with a narrated story or dialogue bring the puppets alive. Puppets may be used to retell a story or to create a new version.

Sock puppets

Take an old sock, some wool, a needle, buttons, pieces of felt, cotton wool, pipe cleaners and invent a sock puppet character. Place a folded small paper plate inside the toe of the sock to act as a mouth.

Shadow puppets

Cut out a body shape with movable arms and legs fixed to the body part with tape or clips. The body and movable limbs can be attached by tape to sticks. Shadow puppets work best when their shadow is reflected from a light onto a screen made from a white sheet.

Paper bag puppets

Take a large paper bag and glue on hair, eyes, mouth, and nose from wool, cloth, paper, or other scraps.

Finger puppets

A figure is made from cardboard and scraps are glued to the cardboard to make facial features and clothes. A band of paper holds the puppet on to the finger.

Glove puppets

Up to five characters can be made in a glove puppet. Cut out figures from cardboard, decorate and glue or tape to a glove.

Paper plate puppets

Take a paper plate, decorate and attach to a stick.

Papier-mâché puppets

Inflate a balloon and cover with layers of paper soaked in glue. When dry, the balloon is popped and the head of the puppet is painted.

A diorama illustrating a favorite part of a book.

MODELS AND DESIGNS

➡ Make **models** or **dioramas** about stories read. Simple Plasticine figures placed in painted shoe boxes are most effective. Discuss the models.

➡ Design **jackets** for books read in class. First, read or tell the story to the class and cover over the book jacket so children are not influenced by the illustrator's views of the story. Compare and contrast children's book jackets with those of the author or illustrator.

➡ Draw a **map** relating to the story, for example, the farm yard in *Charlotte's Web* or the land behind the wardrobe in *The Lion, the Witch and the Wardrobe*. Explain the map to others in the class.

➡ **Act out** stories such as *Where the Wild Things Are*. Children may take Polaroid photographs of the display, then the photographs may be displayed in the correct story sequence.

READER'S THEATER

Children write scripts from a story which can be performed with puppets or with no props at all. Basically, it involves a group of children reading in a circle the scripts they have devised based on familiar stories such as *Little Red Riding Hood* or *The Three Bears*. After they have grasped the idea of devising script-like dialogue to tell the story, children may develop reader's theater scripts based on chapters of a novel or from their own stories.

An easy way to begin reader's theater is to provide children with copies of a short story. Various children take it in turn to read the dialogue and the narration. This activity can be practiced until it is word perfect and then performed for an audience. After children have practiced the easy form of reader's theater, the exercise of writing scripts for the dialogue and narration sections of a story can begin.

Reading scripts prepared for reader's theater.

STORYTELLING

Teachers are often storytellers in the classroom but the simple techniques of good storytelling can be taught to children and it then becomes a means of oral response to literature. Children may choose to retell favorite stories to children in the class or to younger children in the school.

There are important steps in storytelling.

1. **Choosing the story**
   The story must fit the audience and create the appropriate mood. Simple plots are easiest to remember.

2. **Preparing the story for telling**
   Mem Fox (1980) suggests that nothing kills the joy of storytelling faster than a speaker who is sweating with terror in case she forgets the words. So do not learn the story off by heart and word by word.

Mem Fox suggests reading the story several times, then telling it to a wall or mirror. Some storytellers tape-record their stories and others try them out on their family or friends before telling them to a different audience. Some storytellers jot down notes so that the plot and characters' names are remembered. Remember to learn the first line of the story by heart though, so that you get off to a good start.

3. **Beginnings and endings**

   Many stories begin with "Once upon a time..." or "Long, long ago..." encouraging children to work out a suitable beginning and a good ending. Mem Fox often completes her stories with "Four, six, eight, ten, that's all. Amen!"

4. **Telling the story**
   - ➡ Make sure everyone can hear and see. It is best if people sit in a group and the storyteller sits in with them.
   - ➡ Use a prop to begin, or relate something about the author or discuss a related event.
   - ➡ Maintain eye contact with the audience, open eyes wide for effect.
   - ➡ Vary the tone and volume of the voice.
   - ➡ Vary facial expressions and gestures.
   - ➡ Conclude the story slowly so that the audience has the feeling of completeness.

Written responses to literature

Some teachers set up writing folders where students can respond to the books they have read. The folders are based on the idea of dialogue jour-

nals where children write down their ideas and thoughts about books and the teacher reads them and adds comments (but never grades the observations). Often these journals or folders are private and available only to the child to read. Writing folders may include loose leaves of paper or a small booklet.

Sharing response journals.

Nancie Atwell claims that writing allows for a kind of reflection not generally possible with speech, and therefore written responses to books are more sustained and considered than oral conferences. A further consideration is the possible important connections students might make between what they read and what they write. Nancie supplies each of the twelve- to thirteen-year-old students in her class with a folder containing a letter bearing these instructions:

> This folder is a place for you and me to talk about books, reading, authors and writing. You're to write letters to me and I'll write back to you.
>
> In your letters to me, talk with me about what you've read, tell me what you thought and felt and why, tell me what you liked and didn't like and why, tell me what these books meant to you and said to you. Ask me questions or for help, and write back to me about my ideas, feelings and questions.
>
> (Atwell 1984, p. 242)

After a year of writing about reading, one student in Nancie Atwell's class wrote:

> I as a writer, learned to write by reading, writing, listening to other people's writing and discussing my writing.
>
> The way reading helps me is when I 'open up' a book I've read. To do this I sort out the parts I like and don't like and decide why. I notice how the author started, ended and tied the middle together. Then I look for good describing words and the way thoughts and feelings are used. I try to decide whether or not a book is 'good' for me. A good book is one that I enjoy, one that fully takes me into another world, one that is believable, one that I get so caught up in I want to finish it and one that I can picture in my mind.
>
> When I finish a book, if I can go back and picture different parts, I know the author added many details and descriptions. This is something I try to do with my own writing.
>
> My reading log has also been a big help. Talking (writing) has helped me to understand reading and writing much more than I used to.

Very often the content of literature becomes the subject matter of stories written by children. Children may take ideas from a plot and modify them in their own stories. They may innovate and create stories just a little removed from stories they have heard. For example, children may write a story about three sheep crossing a bridge with a fierce dragon under the bridge (modeled on *The Three Billy Goats Gruff*). Alternatively, children may respond to stories by creating new and different endings, new characters and events. The sky's the limit.

At times, links to particular stories may be hard to trace. Often, several stories come together in children's responses through drama, art, music, and so on. The more children are encouraged to take time over a book, the longer they contemplate the story, the richer the response will be.

WAYS OF ENCOURAGING RESPONSE THROUGH WRITING [1]

➡ Compile class or group stories based on a story read in class. Many teachers encourage children to innovate, that is, use the same underlying structure as a story they have read, but change the vocabulary. For example, try this idea based on a story by Bill Martin:

> Brown Bear, Brown Bear,
> What did you see? (old version)

and change it to

> Black dog, Black dog,
> What did you see? (new version)

or

> What good luck.
> What bad luck. (old version)

or

> How fortunate the boat could sail.
> How unfortunate the sail had a hole in it. (new version)

➡ Set up class journals, poems, or stories about books read. In this way, children can also share ideas about reading with others.

➡ Write continuous stories. Perhaps begin reading a story, leave out the ending so children can write alternative endings.

➡ Write a letter to a friend in the class, recommending a certain book. Make sure the reasons for recommending it are clearly explained.

➡ Write a new ending to the story.

➡ Write letters to the librarian requesting the purchase of particular books. These books may be based around children's interest, for example sport, hobbies, or pets.

➡ Write sets of questions about the books read. These can be compiled to make sets of Trivial Pursuit questions.

➡ Write personal reactions to books to read aloud to the class. These reactions can be stapled together to make a book for the library.

➡ Write additional adventures of a character in a book.

➡ Write a letter to parents explaining why a book should be purchased for birthday or Christmas presents.

---

1. For more writing activities, see Coody and Nelson, 1982.

➼ Children's books can act as models for writing. Read *Penny Pollard's Diary* by Robin Klein to the class and encourage children to keep a diary written in the same style as Penny's. *Penny Pollard's Letters*, also by Robin Klein, is written in letter style and this could also act as a model for children who want to write letter style journals.

➼ Children may keep a writing journal in which they write down their responses to the books they read.

Alternatively, the journal can be divided into two columns. In one column children write the main events in the story and in the other column their responses .

Main events	Response
Max was angry.	I felt sorry for him.
His room changed.	This was scary.
He was king of the wild things.	I would like to be King Foo.

➼ Allow children to try writing in a range of genres themselves after reading a variety of literature, for example: fairytales, myths, legends, fables, poetry, and animal stories.

Using other media for response

After reading a book children may use any of the following media to respond to the book.

FILM OR VIDEOTAPE

Children may film an extension of the story, a favorite part, an in-depth look at some of the characters, a parody of the story. In a parody of, for example, *Cinderella*, a present-day version of the old fairytale may be developed. Some stories can be made into melodramas with boys acting as girls and vice versa. Scripts will be written describing setting and action and organized well before filming the performance.

PHOTOGRAPHS

A story may be told in photographs. Children may dress up and act out the story as others photograph the plot. The photographs may be accompanied by brief written descriptions or by tape-recording of events.

RADIO PLAY

In making a radio play, the plot of the story and the words and actions of the characters become the information for the radio play script (similar to reader's theater). Children write the script, include music and sound effects and then broadcast the completed play over the school's public address system.

SLIDE/TAPE PRESENTATIONS

Students may make slide/tape presentations in several ways.

1. Picture-book slide/tape displays can be produced from slides made of picture books. Children can read the text of the story, along with appropriate sound effects, onto a tape.

2. Slides can be made of children's drawings. The tape can contain the story outline.

3. Slides can be made of children dressed up as book characters acting out events. The characters may be dressed up in clothes appropriate to the place and setting.

If slides are not available, then illustrations drawn on overhead projector film will work nearly as well.

Models, dioramas, maps, paintings, collage, and paper mosaic models are all media children can use in responding to the ideas in books.

Music and drama discussion groups are also valuable aids in eliciting children's responses.

The following suggestions present alternatives to a written book report. A selection of these ideas may be included on a chart displayed in the

	Book title and comment	Tick Date
Write to a character in the book.		
Talk to the teacher about the book.		
Write a newspaper advertisement for the book.		
Build a model of an important object in the story.		
Change your story into a comic strip.		
Make a map of the story or parts of the story.		
Prepare a page for oral reading and tape it.		
Send a letter to a friend describing the book.		
Use the overhead projector.		

One alternative to a written report: a vertical chart.

classroom in a spinning wheel or vertical chart. Children may opt for a variety of activities in which to respond to the books they have read. One response may be: "I want to read. another book," which should be encouraged. After all, the aim of the program is to develop keen readers.

Another alternative to a written report: a wheel chart

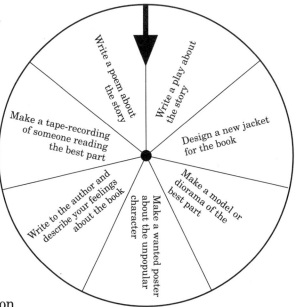

101 alternatives to written book reports

1. Make a puppet based on a character in the story.
2. Draw a map or plan based on part of the story.
3. Arrange a book fair based on books by favorite authors. Work with a local bookstore to do this.
4. Prepare a version of the story to read aloud to younger children.
5. Construct a mobile of the book's characters.
6. Build a model of a favorite part of the story.
7. Invent mixed-up word puzzles from key words in the book.
8. Make a wanted poster for a character in the book.
9. Write a poem about the story.
10. Talk to the teacher about your book.
11. Select a short passage to read aloud.
12. Write a letter to the publisher giving impressions of the book to spread the word.
13. Send a letter to a friend to spread the word about the book.
14. Write a newspaper advertisement for the book.
15. Rewrite part of the book as a radio play.
16. Prepare a page for oral reading and tape-record.
17. Make transparencies about the story to use with the overhead projector.
18. Change your story into a comic strip.
19. Write a radio play about the story.
20. Make up a reader's theater script for the story.
21. Design a new jacket for the book.
22. Write to the author describing your feelings about the book.
23. Construct an author mobile showing the titles and illustrations of the books by the author.
24. Make a frieze to illustrate the book.
25. Write a personality description of a book character.

26. Make a book scene out of burlap and felt.
27. Make individual or class rating charts for books read.
28. Make a "sandwich board" poster to describe a book.
29. Arrange a display of artifacts to accompany a book.
30. Illustrate the book using a variety of art techniques.
31. Make a book scene from mosaic or collage cut from magazines.
32. Paint life-size characters from a book (trace around each other).
33. Make an illustrated time line of events occurring in the book.
34. Construct a table-top model of the setting and characters.
35. Compose a fable from the book.
36. Conduct a book auction where books are described and sold.
37. Rewrite the story as a modern day melodrama or soap opera.
38. Develop a crossword puzzle based on names and events in the book.
39. Prepare a book-of-the-week display.
40. Make a stained glass window depicting a book scene using tissue paper and cellophane.
41. Write a television commercial advertising the book.
42. Make a list of quotations from the book and display.
43. Pretend you are one of the characters and write a letter to the class.
44. Make illustrated bookmarks.
45. Make a cumulative book review by adding a sentence as students finish chapters of a book.
46. Conduct a panel discussion of books read.
47. Dress up in costume as book characters and hold a parade.
48. Write an imaginary autobiography of a book character.
49. Construct shadow puppets and a shadow theater.
50. Write a new ending to an old story.
51. Prepare a paper scroll depicting the story events.
52. Compare and contrast two book characters.
53. Construct a game of Trivial Pursuit using book events and characters in your questions.
54. Make story characters from felt for the felt board.
55. Play literature quiz games with three contestants and an announcer, similar to "Jeopardy."
56. Write a class play based on a book and perform it for another class.
57. Carve story characters from bars of soap.
58. Model book characters from clay or Plasticine.
59. Paint a poster of a story scene.
60. Organize a treasure hunt using book clues.
61. Write a literature newsletter.
62. Compile an imaginary diary that may be kept by a book character.
63. Dress dolls in costume to create a storybook family.
64. Write an additional chapter of a book.
65. Make placemats of book characters and laminate them.

66. Write a parody of a book. The parody could be a melodrama.
67. Make a videotape of children acting out the story.
68. Make a slide/tape production of children acting out the story.
69. Write an imaginary letter between two characters in a book.
70. Prepare a series of reader's theaters to perform for parents.
71. Create paper mosaics for story scenes.
72. Write a newspaper article based on a story episode.
73. Play book-title charades.
74. Plan storytelling sessions for younger children.
75. Plan and make a board game, similar to Monopoly but using a map of the story events.
76. Make a series of cloze procedure sentences for a friend to fill in.
77. Make a Choose-Your-Own-Adventure book based on the book read.
78. Interview a book character and either write or tape the interview.
79. Look through the book for stereotypes, for example: studious—glasses; cheeky—red hair.
80. Jumble the sentences in a story for others to reassemble.
81. Set up a classroom comment sheet where children can write ideas.
82. Make a list of Who's Who in a story and illustrate.
83. Cut out shapes depicting characters and use with the overhead projector.
84. Make a chalkboard frieze of the most interesting event.
85. Make up a story bag where key items form the story are kept and show these as you retell the story.
86. Make finger puppets of book characters.
87. Make newspaper headlines based on the story.
88. Decorate storage bins and wastepaper baskets with illustrations from the story.
89. Compile a list of figurative language from the book.
90. Plan to cook something mentioned in the book.
91. Make a big Shared Book based on the book.
92. Construct a flip book depicting scenes from the book.
93. Make a crazy mixed-up book where pages are cut in half and characters combined in various ways.
94. Make a mask of a character in the book.
95. Write a publisher's blurb to sell the book.
96. Make a rebus of a short story and try it out with others.
97. Write a letter to the librarian suggesting why he or she should or should not recommend the book to others.
98. Dress paper dolls as book characters.
99. Look up the biography of the author and tell others about the books written.
100. Compose a telegram about the book, then extend it to an overnight telegram of fifty words.
101. Role-play book characters and children guess the character.

THE AUTHOR
AND ILLUSTRATOR

4

Finding out about authors and illustrators helps children learn that books are created by real living people. Many authors have recorded their autobiographies in journals such as *Language Arts* or *The Horn Book Magazine*. It is possible to find out

- ➡ how the author came to write stories
- ➡ what techniques the author has used
- ➡ how the author's individual style has developed

Some authors encourage their readers to write to them and share ideas about books. The author may also suggest further books for children to read or share ideas about writing. By displaying photographs of authors, information about them and a descriptive list of books written by particular authors, children are then able to follow through a series of books written by their favorites. Just as adults often find one or two authors enjoyable at particular times, children also like to read all the books by Judy Blume or Colin Thiele, for example.

The following brief biographies provide information about authors listed by children, librarians, and teachers as some of the most popular with primary school children.

ALLAN AND JANET AHLBERG

Allan and Janet Ahlberg are a literary team—he writes, she illustrates, together they design. "We are book makers rather than author and illustrator," says Allan. "What matters to us is the printed bound object, the whole book, cover to cover." Collaborators since the early 1970s, their books are unique because of the sense of unity each possesses—a unity usually only achieved when the writer and illustrator are the same person.

Well known for their many picture books, comic tales, and rhyming stories, their works are based on lighthearted fun, clear morals, and happy endings. Many of their books, such as *Peepo!*, focus on the simplicity and joy of everyday objects and events while revealing a world of fascinating sights for preschoolers. They often use classic fairy-tale characters in their stories. In *Jeremiah in the Dark Woods,* for example, the boy detective embarks on a journey that introduces him to three bears and takes him

Photo: Michael Stockton

past a field of giant beanstalks. *The Jolly Postman* features a postman who delivers letters to the likes of Cinderella and Goldilocks. The work provides the letters and reflects the originality of their collaborations.

Allan, born in England in 1938, was a teacher before he began writing for children full time in 1975. Janet, born in England in 1944, worked as a layout artist and freelance designer before she began to illustrate full time.

Among their many awards is the Greenaway Medal for *Each Peach Pear Plum.*

Janet and Allan Ahlberg live and work together in London, England. They have several works in progress. They can be contacted c/o Viking Children's Books, 375 Hudson Street, New York, NY 10014-3657.

SELECT BIBLIOGRAPHY

Burglar Bill (1977)

Jeremiah in the Dark Woods (1977)

The Little Worm Book (1979)

Each Peach Pear Plum (1979)

Funnybones (1980)

The Ha Ha Bonk Book (1982)

The Baby's Catalogue (1982)

The Jolly Postman (1986)

The Cinderella Show (1986)

Starting School (1988)

The Clothes Horse and Other Stories (1987)

The Bear Nobody Wanted (1993)

It Was a Dark and Stormy Night (1994)

The Giant's Baby

LLOYD ALEXANDER

Lloyd Alexander is considered one of the world's master storytellers. Although he is best known as a writer of fantasy, he believes fantasy is just one of many ways to express attitudes and feelings about real people, real human relationships and problems. "Writing realism or fantasy," he says, "my concerns are the same: how we learn to be genuine human beings."

Lloyd knew he wanted to be a writer by the time he was fifteen, although, he says, "I had no idea how to become an author." When he did not learn enough at college to be one, he opted for adventure. He joined the military during World War II, and as a member of an American combat intelligence team, he was sent to Wales to finish his training. This country seemed like an enchanted kingdom and, years later, greatly influenced his writing.

Lloyd returned to the United States after the war. To earn a living he worked as a cartoonist, advertising writer, layout artist, and editor for a small magazine. In his spare time he wrote adult fiction. It was several years before he began writing for young people —a creative and liberating experience, he says, for it was in writing for young people that he could best express his own feelings.

Lloyd is perhaps best known for the five books in his Prydain Chronicles, most of which focus on the battle between his good and evil characters. Among his many award-winning books are *The High King*, from the Prydain series, which won the Newbery Medal in 1969.

Portrait by Trina Schart Hyman

Lloyd Alexander was born in Philadelphia, Pennsylvania, in 1924. Today he lives in Drexel Hill near Philadelphia, where he writes and continues to do drawings, cartoons, and etchings for his own enjoyment. He can be contacted c/o Dutton Children's Books, 375 Hudson Street, New York, NY 10014-3657.

SELECT BIBLIOGRAPHY

Time Cat (1963)

The Prydain Chronicles (1964-1973)

The Truthful Harp (1967)

The Marvelous Misadventures of Sebastian (1970)

The King's Fountain (1971)

The Cat Who Wished to Be a Man (1973)

The Wizard in the Tree (1975)

The First Two Lives of Lukas-Kasha (1978)

The Westmark Trilogy (1981-1984)

The Vesper Holly Adventures (1986-1990)

The Remarkable Journey of Prince Jen (1991)

The Fortune-tellers (1992)

BETSY BYARS

Betsy Byars is best known for her stories about ordinary events, involving children who eventually solve their particular problems. She presents her characters realistically and objectively. She does not tell the reader what is right and wrong; the reader has to judge whether the characters have behaved appropriately.

Photo: Bashnan Studios

Most of her books grow out of everyday experiences—something that really happened, a newspaper story, an event from her children's lives. The inspiration for *The Summer of the Swans,* for example, came from her experiences as a volunteer of mentally challenged children. *The Pinballs,* one of her most popular books, tells the story of three children living together in a foster home. *The 18th Emergency* also deals with children's relationships and how their problems are solved.

Betsy says her first inclination was to write mystery stories. As her children grew, however, she became more and more interested in writing for children. "I'm sure I would never have written my books if I had not had children…they were very communicative kids, always wanting to tell me where they had been and who said what, and all of that was very helpful."

She has learned, she says, not to write down to her readers. "I must write up to them…I am always impressed to find out how many of them are writing stories and how knowledgeable they are about writing."

Betsy has written several award-winning books. Among her awards is the Newbery Medal in 1971 for *The Summer of the Swans*. Her novels have been translated into several languages and many have been dramatized on television.

Betsy was born in North Carolina in 1928. She graduated from Queens College with a B.A. in English. Currently, she lives in Clemens, South Carolina where she continues to write. She can be contacted c/o Viking Children's Books, 375 Hudson Street, New York, NY 10014-3657.

SELECT BIBLIOGRAPHY

The Midnight Fox (1968)

Trouble River (1969)

The Summer of the Swans (1970)

The House of Wings (1972)

The 18th Emergency (1973)

The Lace Snail (1975)

The TV Kid (1976)

Good-bye, Chicken Little (1979)

The Night Swimmers (1980)

The Two-Thousand-Pound Goldfish (1982)

The Computer Nut (1984)

The Blossoms Meet the Vulture Lady (1986)

Beans on the Roof (1988)

The Burning Questions of Bingo Brown (1988)

Hooray for the Golly Sisters! (1990)

Wanted…Mud Blossoms (1991)

Coast to Coast (1992)

McMummy (1993)

BEVERLY CLEARY

Writing for young readers, Beverly Cleary says, was her childhood ambition. "As a child I had difficulty learning to read. The discovery, when I was about eight years old, that I could actually read, and read with pleasure, was one

Photo: Sandra Hansen

of the most exciting moments of my life. From that moment on, as I read through the library shelves, I searched for, but was unable to find, the books I wanted to read most of all: books about the sort of children who lived in my neighborhood, books that would make me laugh. The stories I write are the stories I wanted to read as a child, and the experience I hope to share with children is the discovery that reading is one of the pleasures of life and not just something one must do in school."

Her first book, *Henry Huggins,* is based on an amusing incident about two children who had to take their dog home on a street-car. After writing several books about Henry and his friends, Beverly was asked why she didn't write similar stories for girls. She took the suggestion to heart and wrote *Fifteen.*

In a writing career that has spanned over four decades, Beverly is perhaps best known for her well-loved character Ramona—the Ramona books have served as an introduction to the novel for many young readers advancing beyond picture books. The humorous, everyday dilemmas of all the Ramona books strike a chord with children—and amuse at the same time.

Beverly has numerous awards during her illustrious writing career, including the Newbery Medal in 1984 for *Dear Mr. Henshaw.*

Beverly was born in Oregon in 1916. A graduate of the University of California and University of Washington, she was a librarian before becoming a writer. Currently, she lives in northern California. She can be contacted c/o Morrow Junior Books, 1350 Avenue of the Americas, New York, NY 10019.

SELECT BIBLIOGRAPHY

Henry Huggins (1950)

Henry and Beezus (1952)

Henry and Ribsy (1954)

Beezus and Ramona (1955)

Fifteen (1956)

Emily's Runaway Imagination (1961)

Ribsy (1964)

Henry and the Clubhouse (1962)

The Mouse and the Motorcycle (1965)

Runaway Ralph (1970)

Ramona the Brave (1975)

Dear Mr. Henshaw (1983)

Ramona Forever (1984)

The Growing-up Feet (1987)

Strider (1991)

Petey's Bedtime Story (1993)

ROALD DAHL

Roald Dahl's children's fiction is known for its sudden turns into the fantastic, its wheeling, free-moving, fast-moving pulse, and its decidedly harsh treatment of any adult foolish enough to cause trouble for the young heroes and heroines.

He always maintained that children are more vulgar than grownups, have a coarser sense of humor, and are more cruel. He often commented that the key to his success as a children's writer was that he conspired with them against adults.

James and the Giant Peach, for example, tells about a young boy who travels thousands of miles in a house-sized peach, after the giant peach crushes his aunts. In *Matilda*, the headmistress who deals with unruly children by grabbing them by the hair and tossing them out windows, is finally banished by Matilda. In *The*

Witches, the young boy thwarts witches who are planning to kill all the children in England.

Roald's career as a children's writer began when he started making up bedtime stories for his own children. "Children...are highly critical," he once said. "You have to keep things ticking along...You have to know what children like."

Sales of his books reflect his continued popularity. *Charlie and the Chocolate Factory* and *Charlie and the Great Glass Elevator* have sold more than one million hardcover copies in the United States and *James and the Giant Peach* more than 350,000 copies. *Charlie and the Chocolate Factory* was voted one of the best-loved children's books of all time. His many awards and honors include both the New York Times Outstanding Books Award and the Whitbread Award in 1983 for *The Witches.*

Roald was born in South Wales in 1916 and died in Oxford, England in 1990.

SELECT BIBLIOGRAPHY

James and the Giant Peach (1961)

Charlie and the Chocolate Factory (1964)

Fantastic Mr. Fox (1970)

Charlie and the Great Glass Elevator (1972)

Danny, The Champion of the World (1975)

The Wonderful Story of Henry Sugar and Six More (1977)

The Enormous Crocodile (1978)

The Twits (1980)

The BFG (1982)

Revolting Rhymes (1983)

The Witches (1983)

Boy: Tales of Childhood (autobiography) (1984)

Matilda (1988)

Rhyme Stew (1989)

The Vicar of Nibbleswicke (published posthumously, 1992)

MEM FOX

Mem Fox wrote the first draft of *Possum Magic,* her first book, in 1978, as an assignment when she was a mature-age student of children's literature. Rejected nine times over five years, it was finally published in 1983 and is the best-selling children's book in Australia's history. Since then, she has written eighteen picture books for children and four books for adults on literacy and drama teaching.

Her ideas for books, she says, come from her own life. *Sophie* and *Wilfrid Gordon McDonald Partridge,* for example, were inspired by the close relationship she had with her grandfather. *Koala Lou* (her personal favorite) arose from her own position as the eldest of three sisters.

Mem has been writing since she was ten years old. Writing is, however, her second love, she admits. Her first is teaching—something she has been doing since 1973. She continues to write for children, she says, because of the heart-warming reactions she has had to each book as it has been published.

Mem has received several awards for children's literature including the medal of the Order of Australia.

Photo: The Photography Studio

Mem was born in Melbourne, Australia in 1946. At the age of six months she went to Africa with her parents and grew up on a mission in Zimbabwe. She is a graduate of the Rose Bruford Drama School in London, England, the South Australian College of Advanced Education, and Flinders University in Adelaide, Australia where she is now a senior lecturer in Language Arts. Currently, she and her husband live in Adelaide. She can be contacted c/o Harcourt Brace & Co., 525 B St. #1900, San Diego, CA 92101-4495.

SELECT BIBLIOGRAPHY

Possum Magic (1983)

Wilfrid Gordon McDonald Partridge (1984)

Hattie and the Fox (1986)

Koala Lou (1987)

Night Noises (1988)

Guess What? (1988)

Shoes From Grandpa (1988)

Sophie (1988)

Feathers and Fools (1988)

Time for Bed (1993)

Tough Boris (1994)

TED HARRISON

Ted Harrison's writing career was born out of necessity. "I was teaching grade-two Cree children in northern Alberta when I first arrived in Canada," he says. "There were no books available showing the local native culture so I

illustrated my own in felt pen. The kids supplied the ideas." The book was called *A Northern Alphabet*.

Since that time, Ted has written and/or illustrated six more books for both adults and children. *The Last Horizon*, which includes poetry, is geared toward older children and adults. *The Northern Alphabet* and *Children of the Yukon* are for children learning to read. They have also been used by adult immigrants learning English.

Considered one of Canada's most prominent artists, Ted continues to write and illustrate children's books, he says, "because I taught school for twenty-nine years and have an interest in the encouragement of literacy and literature amongst youth." His ideas come from his environment and his experiences, plus a touch of imagination and fantasy. He has become a primary interpreter of Canada's north, for both Canadian and international audiences.

Ted's work has earned him numerous awards and honors. *Children of the Yukon* was chosen A Child Study Association's Best Children's Book in 1977. *The Cremation of Sam McGee*, which he illustrated, was an American Library Association Notable Book and a New York Times Best Book Selection. In 1987 Ted received the Order of Canada.

Ted was born in Wingate, England in 1926. He received a classical art education at Hartlepool College and an Art Teacher's Diploma from King's College, University of Durham. After traveling and living around the world, he settled in the Yukon in 1968. In 1993 he and his wife Nicky moved to Victoria, British Columbia, where he continues to write and paint. He can be reached c/o Kids Can Press, 29 Birch Ave., Toronto, ON M4V 1E2.

SELECT BIBLIOGRAPHY

Written and Illustrated:

Children of the Yukon (1977)

A Northern Alphabet (1982)

The Last Horizon (1980)

The Blue Raven (1989)

O Canada (1992)

Illustrated:

The Cremation of Sam McGee (1986)

The Shooting of Dan McGrew (1988)

MONICA HUGHES

"I cannot remember a time when I was not either dreaming of or struggling to be a writer," says Monica Hughes. Still, it was not until after her children started school that she looked to writing as a career possibility. At first, she wrote with an adult audience in mind. After she was commissioned to com-

pose a historical novella for grade school use, however, she began to write almost exclusively for children and young adults.

Best known for her science fiction, Monica also writes realistic and historical fiction. She finds her ideas everywhere. An explosion at an Edmonton generating station inspired *Beyond the Dark River*. The Isis trilogy, her best-known science fiction work for young people, was influenced by David, the boy who had to live in a glass bubble. She wrote *Devil on My Back* after reading a magazine article on computer technology.

Throughout Monica's works, the themes of isolation and search for identity prevail. Her writings have also been greatly influenced by her interest in astronomy and her fascination for history, art, and the written word. Her early exposure to these and many other intriguing and curious subjects and theories has fueled many of her writings. She maintains individuals can, and should, make a difference and looks back to the ideals of the heroic stories of the nineteenth century to guide people today. She believes a good writer for children helps them to explore the world and the future, and to find acceptable answers to the Big Questions: What's life about? and What is it to be human? "But always," Monica says, "there must be hope."

Monica's books have received numerous honours and awards including the Canada Council Prize for Children's Literature in 1981 for *Guardian of Isis* and in 1982 for *Hunter in the Dark*. In 1983, *Hunter in the Dark* was awarded the American Library Association Young Adult Novel Award.

Monica was born in Liverpool, England in 1925. She spent her early years in Egypt before returning to be educated in England and Scotland. She emigrated to Canada in 1952 and worked for five years at the National Research Council in Ottawa where she tested materials and aircraft and spent endless hours discussing the mysteries of space with co-workers.

Currently, Monica lives in Edmonton, Alberta, where she writes, instructs writing workshops, and travels on author visits. She can be contacted c/o HarperCollins Children's Books, 1995 Markham Road, Scarborough, ON M1B 5M8.

SELECT BIBLIOGRAPHY

Beyond the Dark River (1979)

The Keeper of the Isis Light (1980)

The Guardian of Isis (1981)

The Isis Pedlar (1982)

Hunter in the Dark (1982)

Ring-Rise, Ring-Set (1982)

My Name Is Paula Popowich! (1983)

Devil on My Back (1984)

Blaine's Way (1986)

The Promise (1989)

The Refuge (1989)

Invitation to the Game (1989)

The Crystal Drop (1992)

A Handful of Seeds (1993)

The Golden Aquarians (1994)

PAT HUTCHINS

Regarded by many as an innovative author and illustrator, Pat Hutchins has created more than twenty picture and storybooks for children as well as novels for beginning readers. Her first picture book, *Rosie's Walk*, is considered a modern-day classic.

Pat creates her books by envisioning the words and the illustrations together. She likes writing traditional story lines where there are clear beginnings and satisfying conclusions. "The form is circular," she says. "All is explained." Her illustrations are colorful and stylized, and reflect the humor and warmth of her writings.

Pat says she tries to write about what children say and do. Her ideas come from a variety of sources: her children, their friends, real-life situations. Her writings often instruct as they entertain: her books explore subjects such as counting and the concept of time as well as moral tales. For example, *The Doorbell Rang* teaches about sharing as well as mathematical division when a batch of Mother's cookies must be constantly redivided as guests arrive throughout the afternoon. The idea for *The Very*

Worst Monster came to her when her niece told her she wanted to give her baby brother away. In *Good-night, Owl!*, an owl kept awake by noisy neighbors during the day gets his revenge at night.

Pat has received numerous awards and honors. Many of her books have been adapted as filmstrips and stage productions.

Born in 1942, Pat grew up in the country around Yorkshire, England. She knew at an early age that she wanted to become an artist. She studied at Darlington School of Art, then won a scholarship to Leeds College of Art, where she studied illustration. In 1965, Pat and her husband moved to New York City. Here she showed sample illustrations of her work to publishing houses and was encouraged by Macmillan Publishing to write and illustrate her own children's book. Pat created *Rosie's Walk*.

Photo: Laurence Hutchins

Currently, Pat lives in London, England, where she continues to write and draw. She can be contacted c/o Greenwillow Books, 1350 Avenue of the Americas, New York, NY 10019.

SELECT BIBLIOGRAPHY

Rosie's Walk (1968)

The Surprise Party (1969)

Clocks and More Clocks (1970)

Changes, Changes (1971)

Titch (1971)

Good-night, Owl! (1972)

The Wind Blew (1974)

Happy Birthday, Sam (1978)

One-Eyed Jake (1979)

The Tale of Thomas Mead (1980)

The Very Worst Monster (1985)

The Doorbell Rang (1986)

Which Witch Is Which? (1989)

What Game Shall We Play? (1990)

Tidy Titch (1991)

Silly Billy (1992)

My Best Friend (1993)

MADELEINE L'ENGLE

Madeleine L'Engle has written more than forty books of almost every genre for readers of all ages. She writes children's books, she explains, when she has things to say that adults won't understand. "Children are excited by new ideas; they have not yet closed the doors and windows of their imaginations. Provided the story is a good story and makes them want to keep turning the pages, nothing is too difficult for children."

Photo: Nancy Crampton

Madeleine's respect for and confidence in all children are apparent in her writings. Her heroes are usually not the best looking, smartest, or most popular. And, believing human flaws can be virtues, her characters are shy, stubborn, temperamental, misunderstood. Her stories, while often fantastical, realistically portray the problems of her young readers. They depict children's battles for independence and parents learning to accept the danger of that independence. They show the struggle between good and evil, and how love for friends and enemies alike can conquer all.

Madeleine began writing when she was five years old and has been writing ever since. "I believe the story is our chief vehicle of truth," she says. She has won numerous awards and honors including the 1962 Newbery Medal for *A Wrinkle in Time* and the 1980 American Book Award for *A Swiftly Tilting Planet*. In 1986 she was the recipient of the ALAN Award for outstanding contribution to Adolescent Literature from the National Council of Teachers of English.

Madeleine was born in New York City in 1918. When she was twelve she attended an English boarding school in Switzerland, which eventually inspired her romance novel *And Both Were Young*. After returning to the United States two years later, she completed her secondary education, attended Smith College, wrote two novels that were published, became an actress to improve her skills as a playwright, and met and married the actor Hugh Franklin.

Currently, Madeleine L'Engle lives in New York City and northwestern Connecticut. She continues to write, travel, and lecture extensively.

She can be reached: c/o Cathedral of St. John the Divine, 1047 Amsterdam Avenue, New York, NY 10025.

SELECT BIBLIOGRAPHY

And Both Were Young (1949)
Meet the Austins (1960)
A Wrinkle in Time (1962)
The Moon by Night (1963)
The Arm of the Starfish (1965)
A Wind in the Door (1973)
A Ring of Endless Light (1980)
A Swiftly Tilting Planet (1978)
The Anti-Muffins (1980)
The Sphinx at Dawn (1982)
A House Like a Lotus (1984)
Many Waters (1986)
An Acceptable Time (1989)
The Glorious Impossible (1990)

JEAN LITTLE

Jean Little's love of writing developed at an early age. Encouraged by her father, she had her poetry published while still in her teens. Since her first novel, *Mine for Keeps*, was published in 1962, she has written more than twenty novels, picture books, collections of verse, and two volumes of her autobiography.

The daughter of medical missionaries, Jean was born in Taiwan in 1932 and moved to Canada in 1939. She attended the University of Toronto where she received her B.A. in English Language and Literature. Legally blind since birth, Jean taught school for several years before becoming a full-time writer. Her work with handicapped children, she says, and her teaching at the Utah Institute and at Florida University helped inspire her to write for children. Her characters often deal with physical disabilities or learning to cope with fear or grief. Her unsentimental approach has distinguished her work, which has been praised for its humanism and insight.

Photo: © Heritage Studio

She gets her ideas from her own childhood memories, her family, her imagination, and anywhere else ideas lurk. "Getting the ideas is not the hard part," she says. "Turning them into books is the real challenge."

Jean has been recognized several times for her work. Among her awards are Canadian Library Association Children's Book of the Year in 1985 for *Mama's Going to Buy You a Mockingbird*. In 1993 she was made a Member of the Order of Canada.

Currently, Jean lives in an old stone farmhouse near Elora, Ontario, where she writes with the aid of a talking computer. She speaks at conferences throughout Canada and the United States on writing, children and their reading, and the challenges that face a blind person today, accompanied by her Seeing Eye dog, Ritz. Jean can be reached c/o Penguin Books of Canada Ltd., 10 Alcorn Avenue, Suite 300, Toronto, ON M4V 3B2.

SELECT BIBLIOGRAPHY

Mine for Keeps (1962)
Home from Far (1966)
One to Grow On (1969)
Kate (1971)
From Anna (1972)
Listen for the Singing (1977)
Mama's Going to Buy You a Mockingbird (1984)
Lost and Found (1985)
Different Dragons (1985)
Little by Little (1987)
Stars Come Out Within (1990)
Once Upon a Golden Apple (1991)
Jess Was the Brave One (1991)

LOIS LOWRY

Lois Lowry's books, while varied in content and style, are all based on the same general theme: the importance of human connections. "There is the vital need for humans to be aware of their interdependence, not only with each other but with the world and its environment," she says.

Lois often translates her life into fiction to help others who are encountering similar circumstances. Her first book, *A Summer to Die,* is a fictionalized retelling of the untimely death of her sister, and the effect of such a loss on a family. Childhood memories, as well as her experiences as a mother of four children, inspired her to create the character Anastasia Krupnik, who faces a variety of comic crises in several of her books. She also explores challenging adolescent topics that she feels are important. In *Find a Stranger, Say Goodbye* she documented an adopted child's search for her biological mother.

Lois has been the recipient of several awards and honors. In 1979 she won the International Reading Association Children's Book Award for *A Summer to Die*. In 1987 she won the Boston Globe Horn Book Award and the Golden Kite Award for *Rabble Starkey*. She has twice won the Newbery Medal: in 1990 for *Number the Stars* and in 1994 for *The Giver*.

Lois was born in Hawaii in 1937 and has lived all over the world. The daughter of an army dentist, she was, she says, a solitary child who lived in a world of books and her own imagination. While raising four children, she returned to college, got her degree, went to graduate school, and began to write professionally, fulfilling her childhood dream—a dream sparked when she had endlessly scribbled stories and poems into notebooks.

Lois lives in Cambridge, Massachusetts, where she spends her days reading and writing. "I have grandchildren now," she says. "Because of them, I feel a greater urgency to do what I can to convey the knowledge that we live intertwined on this planet and that our future as human beings depends upon our caring more, and doing more, for one another."

Lois can be contacted c/o Houghton Mifflin, 22 Berkley Street, Boston, MA 02116-3764.

SELECT BIBLIOGRAPHY

A Summer to Die (1977)

Find a Stranger, Say Goodbye (1978)

Anastasia Krupnik (1978)

Autumn Street (1980)

Anastasia Again! (1981)

The 100th Thing About Caroline (1983)

Taking Care of Terrific (1983)

Rabble Starkey (1987)

Anastasia's Chosen Career (1988)

All About Sam (1989)

Number the Stars (1990)

Your Move, J.P.! (1991)

Anastasia at This Address (1991)

Attaboy, Sam! (1992)

The Giver (1993)

MARGARET MAHY

Margaret Mahy has written over a hundred books for a wide variety of ages in a wide variety of genres. Best known for her fantastical adventures, she also writes picture books, novels, nonfiction, poetry, and television scripts.

"I consistently get ideas for stories from events around me, which I may choose to describe in a realistic way or translate into fantasy, but family life is my most constant source of ideas," she says. Her writing is also affected by "certain literary traditions" such as the tall story, pantomine, and the gothic ghost story.

Her children's books are entertaining and thought-provoking. Her books for young adults focus on family relationships and coming-of-age themes through a variety of story-telling methods that range from realism to supernaturalism. For example, in *Memory*, a teenager who wants to forget his early life helps an elderly woman suffering from Alzheimers. In *The Haunting*, a young man learns he is to inherit psychic powers he feels are more of a curse than a blessing. Her ability to combine relevant themes with fantasy is equalled by her non-sexist perspective on roles and relationships. Throughout her books, characters of both sexes are subjected to the same strengths and weaknesses.

Margaret surrounded herself with words from an early age. An avid reader, enthralled by the experiences and mysteries stories contained, she began writing her own stories when she was seven. When she was nineteen, she started writing for children. "Children's books seemed to be an area where fantasy was acceptable and could attain a full maturity." In 1980, after working as a children's librarian for more than twenty years, she became a full-time writer.

Margaret has won several awards and honors. These include the Carnegie Medal in 1982 for *The Haunting* and in 1984 for *The Changeover,* the Esther Glen in 1970 for *A Lion in the Meadow*, and AIM Junior Book Award in 1993 for *Underrunners*. In 1993 she received the Order of New Zealand.

Margaret was born in New Zealand in 1936, where she continues to live. In addition to her writing, she is a regular contributor to whole-language reading programs and does extensive work under Writers in Schools Scheme with the New Zealand Book Council. Margaret can be reached c/o Dial Publishers, 925 Penn Avenue, Pittsburgh, PA 15222.

SELECT BIBLIOGRAPHY

A Lion in the Meadow (1969)

The Haunting (1982)

The Changeover (1984)

The Catalogue of the Universe (1985)

The Tricksters (1986)

Memory (1987)

The Blood-and-Thunder Adventures on Hurricane Peak (1989)

The Great White Man-Eating Shark (1989)

The Pumpkin Man and the Crafty Creeper (1990)

The Seven Chinese Brothers (1990)

Dangerous Spaces (1991)

Keeping House (1991)

Underrunners (1992)

The Three-legged Cat (1993)

A Busy Day for a Good Grandmother (1993)

The Rattlebang Picnic (1994)

CAROL MATAS

Carol Matas says there has always been only one compelling reason for her to write—she loves to tell a good story. Still, she hadn't planned to be a writer; she studied to be an actor. Many of her friends were writers, though, and she was inspired to try her hand at fiction after listening to some of their stories. What began as a hobby is now her full-time occupation.

Whether she is writing science fiction, historical fiction, novels, or plays, her ideas, she says, come from everywhere. "They can come from many different quarters, and I always have at least three different ideas for new books circulating in my head." Each Rebecca book, for example, confronts a subject that was in her mind at the time of writing: *The DNA Dimension* is about genetic engineering; *The Fusion Factor* deals with nuclear war. The idea for *Lisa* came to her after she had read a nonfiction book about the rescue of the Danish Jews during World War II.

Carol's work has received many awards and honors. These include the 1988 Geoffrey Bilson Award for Historical Fiction for Young People for *Lisa* and the Sydney Taylor Award in 1993 for *Sworn Enemies*.

Carol was born in Winnipeg, Manitoba in 1949. She received her B.A. in English from the University of Western Ontario and is a graduate of the Actor's Lab in London, England. Currently, she lives in Winnipeg. In addition to writing, she gives writing workshops and readings at schools. Carol can be reached c/o HarperCollins Children's Books, 1995 Markham Road, Scarborough, ON M1B 5M8.

SELECT BIBLIOGRAPHY

The DNA Dimension (1982)

Zanu (1986)

The Fusion Factor (1986)

Me, Myself and I (1987)

Lisa (1987)

Lisa's War (1989)

Jesper (1989)

Name Kris (1989)

It's Up to Us (1991)

Adventure in Legoland (1991)

The Race (1991)

Sworn Enemies (1993)

Safari: Adventure in Legoland (1993)

Daniel's Story (1993)

The Lost Locket (1994)

TOLOLWA MOLLEL

Tololwa Mollel has been a storyteller for most of his life. Growing up on his grandparent's coffee farm in Tanzania, storytelling was, in an oral culture, a way of life. "From an early age I was trained to appreciate a good story and good storytelling and to tell stories."

Tololwa was drawn to the magic of books at an early age. "I have always been interested in writing, possibly due to my interest in storytelling," he says. He did not begin to write seriously and entertain notions of becoming a writer until 1983, however. And it wasn't until after the birth of his first child that he decided to write for children. "I remember reading to my son some stories that I enjoyed as a kid...and the writer in me appreciating the brilliant simplicity of the tales."

Drama studies and theater experiences influence the way he writes, as he strives for a dramatic sense of characterization, action, and dialogue. He has written mostly picture books, some based on folktales, some original. *The Orphan Boy,* based on a Maasi legend about the planet Venus, explains how Venus appears both in dawn's eastern and evening's western skies, while exploring the themes of loyal affection and broken trust.

A Promise to the Sun is based on an original idea; however, it incorporates the spirit and style of African tales.

Tololwa has received several awards and honors. In 1991, *The Orphan Boy* won The Governor General's Award.

Tololwa was born in Arusha, Tanzania in 1952. There he attended university, where he studied theater and literature. He came to Canada in 1976 for a masters degree in drama, then returned home to lecture and act in theater at the University of Dar es Salaam. In 1986 he returned to Canada. He currently lives in Edmonton, Alberta, where he writes children's books, tells stories, and acts periodically. In addition, he gives presentations and workshops throughout North America on storytelling. He can be contacted c/o Oxford University Press Canada, 70 Wynford Drive, Don Mills, ON M3C 1J9.

SELECT BIBLIOGRAPHY

The Orphan Boy (1990)

Rhinos for Lunch and Elephants for Supper! (1991)

A Promise to the Sun: An African Story (1992)

The King and the Tortoise (1993)

The Princess Who Lost Her Hair: An Akamba Legend (1993)

The Flying Tortoise (1994)

KATHERINE PATERSON

"When people ask me what qualifies me to be a writer for children, I say I was once a child. But I was not only a child," says Katherine Paterson, "I was, better still, a weird little kid."

Katherine was born in China in 1932 to missionary parents from the United States. Between the ages of five and eighteen, she moved more than eighteen times. It was, she says, a childhood that included more than her share of frightening and lonely experiences. It was also a childhood filled with reading and writing.

Photo: Jill Paton Walsh

She did not grow up with dreams of becoming a writer, however. After graduating from college in Tennessee, she taught elementary school for a year before getting her masters degree in Christian education. She then served as a missionary in Japan for four years. Shortly after returning to the United States, she married and started a family. Her writing career began when she was asked to develop school curriculum. "I became a writer then…without ever really formulating the ambition to become one. When the curriculum assignment was completed, I turned to fiction, because that is what I most enjoy reading." In 1973, nine years after she began writing, her first novel, *The Sign of the Chrysanthemum,* was published.

The three major influences in Katherine's writings are her experiences in China and Japan (where she spent four years as a missionary), her adolescence in the American south, and her strong biblical heritage. Her children, too, have had a profound influence on her writing, and have supplied rich source material for her books. *Bridge to Terabithia* was written in an attempt to face the issue of death after her son's best friend was killed. *Jacob Have I Loved* is about sibling rivalry.

Katherine has been the recipient of numerous awards. Among these are the Newbery Medal in 1978 for *Bridge to Terabithia* and in 1981 for *Jacob Have I Loved*.

"My aim as a writer is to engage young readers in the use of a story that came out of me, but which is not mine, but ours," she says. "I don't just want my readers' time or attention. I want their lives. I want their senses, imagination, intellect, emotions, and all the experiences they have known breathing life into the words upon the page. I hope to do my part so well that young readers will delight to join me as co-authors."

Katherine can be contacted c/o Dutton Children's Books, 375 Hudson Street, New York, NY 10014-3657.

SELECT BIBLIOGRAPHY

The Sign of the Chrysanthemum (1973)

Of Nightingales That Weep (1974)

The Master Puppeteer (1976)

Bridge to Terabithia (1977)

The Great Gilly Hopkins (1978)

Angels and Other Strangers (1979)

Jacob Have I Loved (1980)

The Crane Wife (1981)

Rebels of the Heavenly Kingdom (1983)

Come Sing (1985)

Consider the Lilies (1986)

The Tongue-Cut Sparrow (1987)

Park's Quest (1988)

The Tale of the Mandarin Ducks (1990)

Lyddie (1991)

GARY PAULSEN

Gary Paulsen has written over 130 books for children and adults. Although he writes picture books, beginning chapter books, children's and juvenile fiction, and adult fiction, he is best known for his powerful young-adult fiction. An adventurer and lover of nature himself, his books are often set

in wilderness areas and feature teen-agers who arrive at self-awareness by way of experiences in nature—often through challenging tests of their own survival instincts.

Gary's love for books began one cold night when he stepped into a library in a small town in northern Minnesota to get warm. "At first it took me a month to read a book, then two weeks, then a week, pretty soon I was reading two books a week." But, it wasn't until he was working as a field engineer in aerospace departments, tracking deep space probes, that he decided—on a whim—to become a writer.

Without having written so much as a short story, he quit his job and headed for Hollywood. There, using a phony résumé, he found work at a magazine and apprenticed himself to three mentors who taught him how to write.

He writes for young readers, he says, because if there is any hope for the human race, it has to come from young people, not adults. "I decided young people were being let down and I'd try to write artistically for them." But first he set out to meet and talk to as many children as possible in both the United States and Canada. "I estimated when I was approaching the end of my research—my trying to learn—that I actively spoke to over thirty thousand individual boys and girls and another hundred or so thousand in groups."

In addition to a writer, Gary has been many things—teacher, field engineer, editor, army sergeant, actor, director, farmer, rancher, truck driver, trapper, professional archer, singer, and musher, to name a few. Still, he has never forgotten how a librarian changed his life. "I tell young people to read like a wolf eats. Read what they tell you not to read and read when they tell you not to. We're the only species that stores our knowledge, and the way we've chosen to do that is in books and libraries."

Gary is recognized in the United States by the National Council of Teachers of English as one of the most important writers of young adult literature in the world. He has also received many state awards for his work.

Gary was born in 1939. For 21/2 years after World War II, he lived in the Philippines. After returning to the United States, his family travelled constantly; the longest time he spent in any school was five months. It was, he says, an unhappy childhood.

Today, Gary divides his time between northern Minnesota, New Mexico, and a 44-foot sloop he is restoring on the Pacific. He can be contacted c/o Flannery Literary, 34-36 28th Street, #5, Long Island City, NY 11106-3516.

SELECT BIBLIOGRAPHY

Dancing Carl (1983)

Tracker

Dogsong (1985)

Sentries (1986)

Hatchet (1987)

The Crossing (1987)

The Island (1988)

The Voyage of the Frog (1989)

The Winter Room (1989)

The Boy Who Owned the School (1990)

Canyons (1990)

Woodsong (1990)

The Cookcamp (1991)

The River (1991)

The Monument (1991)

The Haymeadow (1992)

Nightjohn (1993)

Dogteam (1993)

Harris and Me (1993)

Sisters / Hermanas (1993)

The Car (1994)

KIT PEARSON

Kit Pearson says she knew she wanted to be a writer when she was twelve years old. Still, she spent much of her early adult life procrastinating while she earned degrees in English, Librarianship, and Children's Literature, and worked as a children's librarian. In 1982, motivated by courses she took at the Simmon's College Center for the Study of Children's Literature in Boston, she began writing. Being a children's librarian confirmed for her that it was children she wanted to write for and to.

Kit is the author of five novels for children ages nine to thirteen. Her ideas, she says, come from memories of her own childhood, from stories people have told her, and from history.

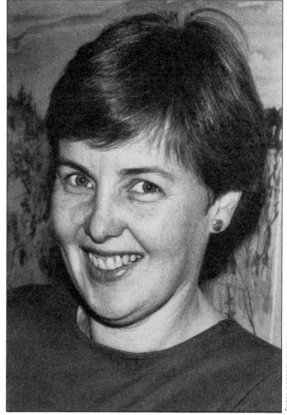

Photo: Russell Kelly

Kit has won numerous awards for her work including the Canadian Library Association's Book of the Year for Children Award in 1988 for *A Handful of Time* and again in 1990 for *The Sky Is Falling*. *The Sky Is Falling* also received Mr. Christie's Book Award in 1990 and the Geoffrey Bilson Award for Historical Fiction for Young People in 1990.

Kit was born in Edmonton, Alberta in 1947. She now lives in Vancouver where she occasionally teaches, and writes books and articles on children's literature and writing for children. Kit can be contacted c/o Penguin Books of Canada Ltd., 10 Alcorn Avenue, Suite 300, Toronto, ON M4V 3B2.

SELECT BIBLIOGRAPHY

The Daring Game (1986)

A Handful of Time (1987)

The Sky Is Falling (1989)

The Singing Basket (1990)
Looking At the Moon (1991)
The Lights Go On Again (1993)

BARBARA REID

Barbara Reid is an illustrator/author who has worked with a variety of mediums for clients in the advertising, educational, and trade book fields. She is best known for her three-dimensional Plasticine illustrations of children's books, including picture books, poetry, and fiction. "I loved reading as a child. I often drew my own pictures to go with my favorite books," she

says. "When I became an illustrator, my favorite projects were for children."

She starts each project by reading the manuscript several times, then surrounding herself with reference materials—music, photographs, fabric, dictionaries, magazines, and so on—that may spark an idea. Once she gets the idea, she plans out her pictures with pencil and paper before putting down the Plasticine. It is a painstaking process. From start to finish, her illustrations for one book can take a year or longer. (In response to the popularity of her Plasticine illustrations, Barbara wrote and illustrated a how-to book for children, *Playing With Plasticine*.)

Barbara has won numerous awards for her illustrations. Among them are the Mr. Christie Book Award in 1991 for the Zoe series, the Ezra Jack Keats Award in 1988 for a body of work including *The New Baby Calf*, and the Elizabeth Mrazik-Cleaver Award in 1987 for *Have You Seen Birds?* and in 1993 for *Two by Two*.

Born in Toronto, Ontario, in 1957, Barbara Reid graduated from the Ontario College of Art in 1980. Currently, she lives in Toronto with her husband and two daughters. While she usually illustrates for other authors, she has written her own books and hopes to continue illustrating her own stories. Barbara can be reached c/o Scholastic Publications, 123 Newkirk Road, Richmond Hill, ON L4C 3G5.

SELECT BIBLIOGRAPHY

Illustrated:

It's Tough to Be a Kid (1983)

The New Baby Calf (1984)

Have You Seen Birds? (1986)

How to Make Pop-Ups (1987)

Have Fun With Magnifying (1987)

Effie (1990)

Gifts (1994)

Written and Illustrated:

Playing With Plasticine (1988)

Zoe's Rainy Day, Zoe's Sunny Day, Zoe's Windy Day,
Zoe's Snowy Day (1991)

Two by Two (1992)

Video:

Barbara Reid: Meet the Author

MAURICE SENDAK

For more than forty years, Maurice Sendak's books have nurtured and been loved by children and adults alike. Recognized as a leading visionary in children's literature, his books have challenged established ideas of

Photo: © Chris Callis

what children's literature is and should be. "Children are willing to deal with many dubious subjects that parents think they shouldn't know about," he says. He is often thought to be the first author/illustrator to deal with the fears that children have of monsters, boredom, jealousy, dreams, and angers.

Maurice's distinctive cross-hatched drawings and elegant paintings have enhanced many authors' works, in addition to his own. In the decade following the success of *A Hole Is to Dig* in 1952, he illustrated more than fifty books, gaining the experience that culminated in *Where the Wild Things Are*, one of the top ten children's book best-sellers of all times.

Among his many awards and honors are the 1964 Caldecott Medal for *Where the Wild Things Are*, the Hans Christian Andersen International Medal in 1970, and the American Book Award in 1982 for *Outside Over There*. In 1990, he was named the first recipient of the Empire State (New York) Award for Excellence in Literature for Children.

Maurice was born in Brooklyn, New York in 1928. He currently lives in Ridgefield, Connecticut, where he has been focusing his attention on the performing arts. In addition, he has formed a national children's theater, which gives him the opportunity to combine all his passions: commissioning and creating original plays, musicals, ballets and operas, as well as developing new productions of existing works. Maurice can be contacted c/o HarperCollins Children's Books, 10 E. 53rd St., New York, NY 10022.

SELECT BIBLIOGRAPHY

Written and illustrated:

Kenny's Window (1956)

Very Far Away (1957)

Alligators All Around (1962)

Chicken Soup With Rice (1962)

One Was Johnny (1962)

Where the Wild Things Are (1963)

Hector Protector (1965)

Higglety Pigglety Pop! (1967)

In the Night Kitchen (1970)

Outside Over There (1981)

We're All in the Dumps (1993)

Illustrated:

Little Bear (1957)

The Moon Jumpers (1957)

Dear Mili (1988)

I Saw, Esau (1992)

JERRY SPINELLI

When Jerry Spinelli was sixteen, his high-school football team won a big game. That night he wrote a poem about it. "The poem was published in the local newspaper, and from then on I wanted to become a writer."

Nearly twenty-five years, four unpublished manuscripts, and hundreds of rejection slips later, his first children's story, *Space Station Seventh Grade*, was published.

Jerry doesn't think of himself writing for children as much as about them. "I hope I write for everyone." He claims no special insights into children or childhood. "Maybe my insights are into myself," he says. "Maybe it's because I tend to be introspective and because there is a part of me that never left the junior-high locker room." His characters are, at an age when most are trying to conform, individualistic, intelligent, daring, and self-reliant.

Jerry believes it is important to "write what you care about" and gets his ideas from everyday life incidents and his own recollections. *Space Station Seventh Grade*, for example, was inspired by a missing lunch. In *There's a Girl in My Hammerlock* he tackles preconceptions about sex roles through the character of Maisie, an eighth-grade girl who joins the school wrestling team. He combines fantasy and real life in *Maniac Magee,* a story about an orphaned boy who encounters prejudice, homelessness, and literacy while searching for a family he can call his own.

In 1991, Jerry was awarded the Newbery Medal for *Maniac Magee.* It is believed this book has won more Readers' Choice state awards than any other book.

Jerry was born in Norristown, Pennsylvania, in 1941. After college, he taught briefly at Temple University but found the job too time-consuming to pursue writing. He found work as an editor of an engineering magazine. It was a job that didn't leave him too exhausted at the end of the day to work on his novels.

Currently, Jerry lives in Phoenixville, Pennsylvania, where he writes full-time. He can be contacted c/o HarperCollins Children's Books, 10 E. 53rd Street, New York, NY 10022.

SELECT BIBLIOGRAPHY

Space Station Seventh Grade (1982)

Who Put That Hair in My Toothbrush? (1984)

Night of the Whale (1985)

Jason and Marceline (1986)

Dump Days (1988)

Maniac Magee (1990)

The Bathwater Gang (1990)

There's a Girl in My Hammerlock (1991)

Fourth Grade Rats (1991)

School Daze: Report to the Principal's Office (1992)

School Daze: Who Ran My Underwear Up the Flagpole? (1992)

School Daze: Do the Funky Pickle (1992)

School Daze: Picklemania! (1993)

JANE YOLEN

Jane Yolen always knew she would be a writer. "The child of writers, I thought all adults became writers," But, she says, her children's book writing career began by accident. A journalist and poet, one day she was asked

if she'd written any books. She hadn't, but answered yes. "To keep from being a liar, I wrote what I assumed would be quick books. Children's books. I have since come to learn that they are about the hardest kind of writing there is."

Jane writes for all ages (including adults) and in all genres including picture books, alphabet and counting rhymes, early readers, science fiction, fantasy, historical novels, nonfiction, music books, and poetry. She is probably best known, though, for her literary folk and fairy tales, drawing on elements of old stories to illustrate modern themes. Ideas, she says, come from everywhere—real-life situations, conversations, newspaper and magazine articles, visuals. *Owl Moon,* for example, is about her husband taking their children owling. *The Girl Who Cried Flowers* was inspired by a Botticelli painting. Her Commander Toad series started when she read an article about a jumping frog contest.

Photo: David Semple

Jane has been widely recognized and honored for her work. Among her many awards is the Caldecott Medal in 1988 for *Owl Moon*.

Jane was born in New York City in 1939. She attended Smith College, where she developed her writing skills. After graduation, she worked for various publishers in New York City. She returned to school in the 1970s, attending the University of Massachusetts where she received a masters of education.

Jane has spoken throughout the United States to children and children's literature groups at schools, libraries, and conferences. Currently, she and her husband live in Massachusetts where she is working on several projects, including poetry anthologies, song books, and novels for children and middle readers. She is also known as a folksinger, critic, essayist, and editor. Jane can be contacted c/o Harcourt Brace, 525 B Street, #1900, San Diego, CA 92101-4495.

SELECT BIBLIOGRAPHY

The Minstrel and the Mountain (1967)

The Emperor and the Kite (1967)

World on a String (1968)

The Girl Who Loved the Wind (1972)

The Girl Who Cried Flowers and Other Tales (1974)

The Little Spotted Fish (1975)

The Transfigured Hart (1975)

The Moon Ribbon and Other Tales (1976)

Dragon's Blood (1981)

The Gift of Sarah Barker (1981)

Heart's Blood (1984)

The Stone Silenus (1984)

Piggins (1987)

The Three Bears Rhyme Book (1987)

Owl Moon (1987)

Here There Be Dragons (1993)

Welcome to the Greenhouse (1993)

Ways of learning about authors

➡ Compare the illustrations of two authors/illustrators, for example, Maurice Sendak and Ezra Jack Keats. Contrast the colors, lines, artistic techniques, characters. Try artwork in a similar style.

Ida played her wonder horn
to rock the baby still –
but never watched.

"Sing!" said the mother.
"We sing," said the three.
So they sang and were glad.
In the hole in the tree.

Illustrations and text by (above) Maurice Sendak and (below) Ezra Jack Keats.

➡ Write a picture book just like one written by a particular author but with one small detail altered. You could change a character in part of the story or even set it in a different place. For example, the story *Ming Lo Moves the Mountain* by Arnold Lobel could be changed by creating a different main character or by making the mountain a tree or a tall building.

➡ Write to an author and find out why and how he or she came to write the book. Names and addresses are provided on pages 23–53.

17 Roberts Row
Winnipeg, Manitoba
R2 M 4R4
June 9, 1994

Dear Jean Little,

How are you? I'm fine. Why did you start to write? My favorite favorite book is *One to grow on.* What is your favorite book you've wrote? In Kindergarten and grade one and grade two I hated to read, but now I love it. I play hardball and I've got twelve homeruns in ten games (The most in the league). Do you think you will write any more books? I hope you do. I love your books!! I know a few too. Mama's going to buy you a *Mockingbird*, *One to grow on*, *Mine for keeps* I've wrote the most books in my class. When I grow up I want to be an author just like you!
Bye-bye.

From,
Tony Petrelli

➡ Close your eyes and listen to part of a story and see if you can guess the author and the book.

➡ Play "Who Am I?" where you become an author and you describe the books you have written. Others must guess who you are.

➡ Complete a chapter. Change part of the chapter and ask children to find the difference in the author's style.

➡ Compile posters of authors. Illustrate them and include important information about the books they have written and information about their likes and dislikes.

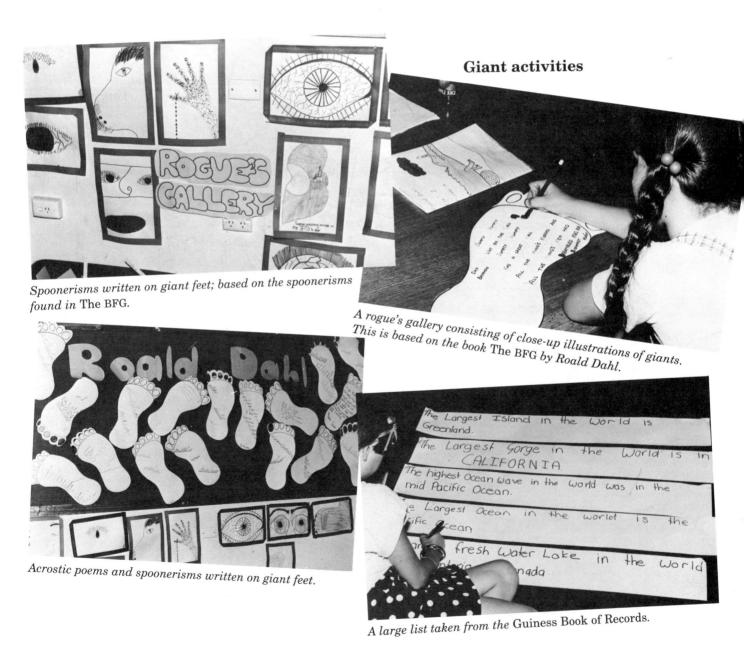

Giant activities

Spoonerisms written on giant feet; based on the spoonerisms found in The BFG.

A rogue's gallery consisting of close-up illustrations of giants. This is based on the book The BFG *by Roald Dahl.*

Acrostic poems and spoonerisms written on giant feet.

A large list taken from the Guiness Book of Records.

➼ Set up a favorite author chart. Each time a person reads a book by an author, award the author with a star. Find the class's favorite author for each school term.

➼ Display the books by one author, for example Betsy Byars. Find out if the books she writes have anything in common, such as characters, plots, or themes.

➼ Take a part from a book by a well-known author. Leave out one paragraph. Rewrite the paragraph in your own words but try to retain the author's writing style.

Classwork based on Roald Dahl's books.

Book review.

Sharing a Roald Dahl book.

Scrambled word puzzle based on titles of books written by Roald Dahl.

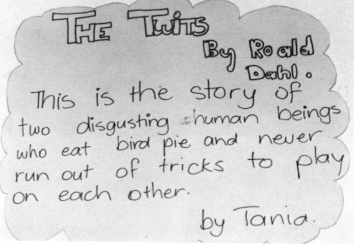

Book reviews.

- Rewrite the final chapter of a book or describe it orally and record it. Try to keep the author's writing style the same.
- Write an autobiography. You are Colin Thiele, Robin Klein, Judy Blume, or another well-known author.
- Illustrate jackets for a selection of books written by one author.

The Lion the Witch and the Wardrobe is really mysterious and weird. It's exciting and there is always something popping up.

Other activities may include the following:

MAGIC MIRROR

Have a cardboard shape and magic mirror in the classroom. Write down the names of several authors or paste up their photographs. Children take turns to describe the books written by the author they like best.

MEET THE AUTHOR

This could be a whole class activity where the children in the class become the audience and one student acts as an interviewer and another student as a favorite author. The interviewer asks questions regarding the kinds of books written, the title of the books, and the plot of a favorite book.

The children in the audience may be invited to guess the name of the author or the activity may be changed by having a child author actually discuss the stories and books he or she has written. This activity could be broadcast over the school's public address system. In order to prepare for this activity children may use the following checklist:

Where were you born?
When were you born?
Where do you live now?
What was the title of your first book?
What experiences have given you ideas for stories?
What part or parts of stories you have written do you like best?
Can you describe your style of writing?
What is your greatest ambition in life?
What is your next book to be about?
What is the secret of your success as a writer?

Author Mem Fox shares her stories with her readers.

AUTHOR PROMOTIONS

Children may act as publishers responsible for advertising and promoting books by particular authors. Discuss various advertising media and the techniques used:

- ➡ television—using videotape
- ➡ radio—using tape-recorder
- ➡ magazine, newspaper
- ➡ posters for bookstores

Drawings of the author, book covers, favorite characters from the authors' books may serve as illustrations. Descriptions of the stories, excerpts from exciting or well-written sections, and lists of books already published may be described to entice the potential reader. Several groups of children may work together to set up author promotions in corners of the classroom or library. Some promotional materials may be gleaned from bookstores on authors such as Roald Dahl, Judy Blume, or Robin Klein.

BOOK PURCHASING COMMITTEE

Organize a book purchasing committee in the classroom. The book selection committee may canvass children in the classroom or children in the school to discover favorite authors and authors children want to read more of.

AUTHOR OF THE MONTH

Send birthday cards with comments about stories to the author or author's publishers on the author's birthday. Read selections of books by the author during the author's birthday month. (Based on an idea from Edwards, 1985.)

January	**July**
Lloyd Alexander January 30, 1924	E.B. White July 11, 1899–1985
February	**August**
Judy Blume February 12, 1938	Paula Danziger August 18, 1944
March	**September**
Patricia McLachlan March 3, 1938	Roald Dahl September 13, 1916–1990
April	**October**
Kit Pearson April 30, 1947	Katherine Paterson October 31, 1932
May	**November**
Gary Paulsen May 17, 1939	Colin Thiele November 16, 1920
June	**December**
Ivan Southall June 8, 1923–	Molly Bang December 29, 1943

PLAY AUTHOR MASTERMIND

This game can be played with two teams of three to eight players. The idea is to match the titles of well-known books with their authors. One team researches ten or twenty titles and authors and within a time limit of three to five minutes asks the other team to match authors' names to stated titles. Then the other team has a turn. Some beginning titles could be:

Title	Author/Answer
The TV Kid	Betsy Byars
The Pinballs	Betsy Byars
Playing Beatie Bow	Ruth Park
Dirty Beasts	Roald Dahl
Tom's Midnight Garden	Philippa Pearce

The Dark Is Rising	Susan Cooper
The Great Gilly Hopkins	Katherine Paterson
I Own the Racecourse	Patricia Wrightson
Hating Alison Ashley	Robin Klein
A Wizard of Earthsea	Ursula Le Guin

Taking part in the "Jeopardy" quiz program with questions based on books by favorite authors.

An alternative would be for one team to name an author and the opposing team to match an author with an appropriate title. The authors could be limited to those on pages 23–53 of this book to begin the activity.

Modify the game by developing authors' Trivial Pursuit where authors, titles, and questions about the events in the story are developed. To narrow the range of authors and titles the game can be played with a selection of books in the classroom.

CLOZE ACTIVITIES

Choose a well-known author such as Judy Blume or Robin Klein and select a favorite section of a book written by her (about one page is enough). Delete every fifth or ninth word. Children complete the cloze exercise by filling in the missing words trying either to remember the story or maintain the author's style:

> The next day we went to the hardware store where my father bought a deluxe power lawn mower. That evening, after our first at-home-in-New-Jersey supper (turkey sandwiches from the local delicatessen), my father went out to cut the grass with his new mower. He did fine on the front, but when _____ got around to the back yard he had

_____ check to see how much grass there was _____ the bag on the mower. It's a very _____ thing to do. The man at the hardware _____ demonstrated just how to do it. Only you _____ to turn the mower off before you reach _____ and my father forgot that.

I heard him _____ "Barbara—I've had an accident!" He ran to _____ house. He grabbed a towel and wrapped it _____ his hand before I had a chance to _____ anything. Then he sat down on the floor _____ turned very pale.

The cloze exercise could be placed on the overhead projector and a large group could work at completing the exercise while discussing why particular words fit the particular author's style of writing.

WRITER'S STYLE

Style involves not only the words an author uses but also the way in which they are arranged to create effects. A writer's style is a very personal matter and authors soon become known for use of particular devices such as:

imagery: appealing to the senses, "as the rain soaked down her stoney face"

personification: "the flowers were dancing"

metaphor: an implied comparison, "he was bearish"

simile: a stated comparison, "like a rose"

connotation: associations by use of words; for example, "*wallowing* rather than *sitting* in the mud"

hyperbole: exaggeration, "she died laughing"

understatement: playing down, "he looked inquisitively at the arrow in his leg"

play on words: "wreading writhing writhmetic"

parody: aping other literature for effect; for example, a modern version of *Cinderella* would be a parody

onomatopoeia: words that sound like their meanings, "splat," "splash"

rhythm: "cats here, cats there, thousands of cats everywhere"

alliteration: repetition of initial consonants, "green grass growing"

assonance: repetition of like vowels, flat, fat, mag wheels

Children can search for metaphors or hyperbole in the work of particular authors providing this does not become an endless tedious task that detracts from the enjoyment of literature. Making charts illustrating interesting uses of words or pointing out the use of words in a particular way may be all that is needed.

THE STORY 5

When using the story approach to teaching literature, children are encouraged to see similarities and differences between stories. Very young children soon recognize that a story has a beginning, a middle, and an end. Older children find that some stories can be classified into various types or genres such as adventure, science fiction, or historical fiction. Children also soon learn about main characters and minor characters, plot, action, and resolutions or conclusions (Lukens 1978). Northrop Frye and Glenna Sloan (1975) have categorized children's stories into four main types. These four main literary structures will be described and then various methods for helping children understand stories follow.

Major literary forms

Northrop Frye's (1964) four basic plot forms are romance, comedy, tragedy, and irony/satire. Sometimes these forms overlap—we have romantic comedies, for example, or romantic tragedies.

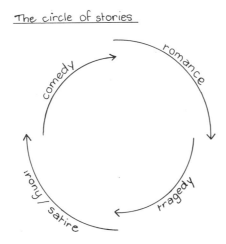

The circle of stories

THE ROMANCE STORY

In the romance story, we usually find a simplified, idealized, brave hero or heroine and an evil villain. Often romance stories are based on the simple **quest** idea where the main character sets out to solve a problem, and after three attempts he or she is successful. At the end of the story the main character returns home wiser, happier, and contented. Some simple romantic quests are found in the Arthurian legends and C.S. Lewis's *Narnia* stories.

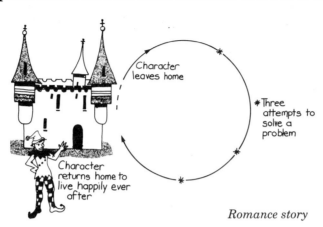

Romance story

COMEDY STORIES

In comedy stories, the hero or heroine is not an idealized type and is often quite frail and fallible like most of us. The hero usually sets out to solve a problem, or perhaps something happens in his or her life that creates a problem to be solved. Bilbo Baggins in *The Lord of the Rings* is a good example of this kind of hero and Wilbur in *Charlotte's Web* is another. Comedy stories always have a happy ending.

TRAGEDY

In these stories the reader often identifies with the tragic character but all along the way we know that fate will bring about a very unhappy ending. Some teachers think tragic stories are unsuitable for young children. Examples of stories in this category are *Shadrack* by Meindert de Jong and *The Silver Sword* by Ian Serraillier.

IRONY AND SATIRE

Again, many teachers do not believe that stories in the irony/satire category are suitable for children. Such stories poke fun at everyday life and show up our foibles. *War and Peas*, the story of a silly war, is a good example. Some people would also see *The Wind in the Willows* or *Watership Down* as satires as they make fun of society with animal characters who act as humans.

The major literary forms—romance, comedy, tragedy, and irony/satire—may be explored with children. Another way of learning about stories is to explore books by category, type, or genre. Many teachers encourage children to read a range of literary genres.

Literary genres

A way of helping children see similarities and differences between stories is to read and classify books according to type or genre. The number of literary genres is limitless and may include

- ➡ adventure
- ➡ science fiction
- ➡ mystery
- ➡ biography
- ➡ non-fiction
- ➡ family stories
- ➡ school stories
- ➡ historical fiction
- ➡ poetry
- ➡ animal stories

Children can also categorize books even further and make up their own genres, for example, detective stories, horse stories, or war stories. John Stewig (1980) and Charlotte Huck (1976) suggest that a literature curriculum in primary schools can best be organized around literary genres. Huck claims that a balanced literature program would be based on a selection of poetry, narrative, non-fiction, realism, and fantasy, and stories set in contemporary, futuristic, and historical settings. Children may be encouraged to keep a record of different genres on charts in the classroom.

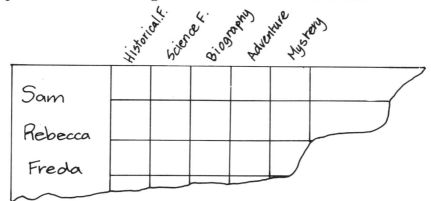

Discovering just what story elements are found in a mystery story or science fiction is an interesting activity for even very young readers.

Story structure

Several teachers claim that if children understand how stories work, then their ability to comprehend them is enhanced. Studying story structure involves teaching children about setting, characters' motives, the plot or action, resolution, and theme.

Elements of story structure

Setting: Where and when does the story take place?
Character's motive: What does the character want to do?
Action: What happens to the character in the story?
Resolution: What happens at the end?
Theme: What is the book telling us?

It is important to remember that discussion of setting, plot, and resolution becomes dull and monotonous if questions such as those shown in the example are continually asked each time a child reads a book. Sometimes children, like adults, merely want to read a book and reflect and not have a barrage of questions to answer. Teachers may discuss the elements of a story—plot, character, setting, theme, author's point of view, or author's style—while incorporating some of the activities described later. Once children have found the setting, character's motives, action, resolution, and theme in simple stories such as *Little Red Riding Hood* or in simple legends such as *Tiddalick*, then this may be all that is necessary and the teacher may not need to discuss these elements further. In fact children often have implicit knowledge of stories as Applebee (1978) found when asking them to tell or retell stories. For more information on elements of story in children's literature, see *A Critical Handbook of Children's Literature* by Rebecca Lukens.

Books with a predictable structure

Children from kindergarten to upper primary grades enjoy books with predictable structures. Some books have a simple, repetitive structure where a line or a verse is added cumulatively as in *This Is the House that Jack Built* or *I Know an Old Woman Who Swallowed a Fly*. In these books children learn the phrases and it becomes easy to say each phrase in order.

Other books with predictable structures include those with predictable plots where things happen in such a way as to enable the reader to predict future events. For example, in the book *Each Peach Pear Plum*, each time we turn a page we expect to find a particular fairytale character. In *What Good Luck, What Bad Luck* the predictable structure of the text gives the reader clues as to what to expect on the next page. Some books with predictable structures use repetition of a particular phrase or sentence, for example, in *May I Bring a Friend* and in the large Read It Again book *What Do You Do?*

Lists of books with predictable structures are being compiled by teacher librarians in many school districts. For a beginning list see Appendix I (page 115).

Literary motifs

Some teachers and children enjoy finding literary motifs in the books they read. A literary motif or literary symbol signifies particular meaning. For example, if a character walks through a forest, the forest signifies a walk into the unknown or that bad or evil events may soon occur. Many stories end happily in the season of spring, which symbolizes rebirth, renewal, and happiness. Glenna Sloan (1975) suggests that literary imagery began with ancient legends, folklore, myths, and legends and that much of this imagery is present in recently published stories. Many stories in fact begin in a summer setting, then evil or a problem befalls the main character in the cold winter and the problem is resolved in spring. Sloan links literary imagery as shown in the diagram at right.

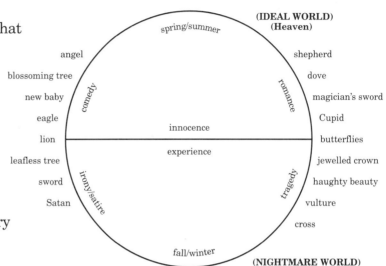

Literary style

Many stories in various literary genres use particular stylistic conventions. Detective stories are usually fast moving and action packed. Science fiction tales are set in another time and place and often contain lots of description to make the setting realistic. Some books are written with rhythm and rhyme to create a mood such as Pamela Allen's book *Bertie and the Bear* and Maurice Sendak's *Where the Wild Things Are*. Literary devices are important components of particular kinds of stories.

When opportunities arise children and teachers may discuss the use of literary devices. They include:

Device	Example
Rhythm and Rhyme	In Wanda Gag's *Millions of Cats*: "Cats here, cats there."
Word play	When Templeton the rat is described as having "no milk of rodent kindness."
Imagery	"the jewel necklace of raindrops."
Metaphor	"he was a bear of a man."
Simile	"as blue as the sea."
Alliteration	"pure purple petal."

Ways of learning about story

EXPLORE LITERARY GENRES

Children write their own stories in various literary genres. Some children may wish to call their story a fairytale, a school story, or an adventure story. Depending on the interests of the children it is possible to develop activities where children write autobiographies (include photographs); fairytales (beginning with "Once upon a time"); funny stories; and sad stories.

DRAMATIZE QUEST STORIES

Use stories such as *The Tale of Peter Rabbit, The Three Billy Goats Gruff*, and *The Three Little Pigs*. They can be made into puppet plays, or full-scale dramatic productions. Creative innovations add a special flavor and make the story belong specifically to the group of children.

CHARACTERS

Cut out examples of good and bad characters from newspapers, TV magazines, comic strips, and magazines. Paste them on large charts.

➡ Children dress up as a favorite book character; as a favorite villain; or as a favorite hero or heroine.

➡ Make up advertisements for characters to be employed in a particular book. The children then have to guess the character. For example:

Situations vacant

Princess wanted, must have white skin, black hair, a good nature and nice clothes. She must be able to get on well with short people, like red apples, pretty hair, and tightly belted dresses. Apply to Queen Frederika, Sneaky Castle.

(or for older children)

Wanted

Small baby who is always in trouble. Must be able to eat whole turtles and mix up stamp collections and destroy everything he can. Apply to Peter, New York.

FAIRYTALE LIMERICKS

Put favorite tales into a different form. For example a fairytale becomes a limerick:

There was a young girl named Snow White
Who was not terribly bright
She fell fast asleep
And was in trouble deep
For many a long day and night

TWENTY QUESTIONS

Pin the name of a book character to the back of a child in the class. The child can ask twenty or forty questions (the children decide on the number) and the class may only answer yes or no. The child must guess the character within the number of questions allocated.

Try these characters:

The Giant from the B.F.G.	Mr. Percival
Gilly Hopkins	Cinderella
Tarzan	Dr. Who
Willy Wonka	Bilbo Baggins
Charlotte	

It may be useful to list the titles of books so that the child who is guessing the character gains a clue. The game can be varied by limiting the characters to ones from fairytales or to those developed by one particular author:

Sleeping Beauty	ugly sister
pig	golden goose
wolf	troll
huntsman	Goldilocks
Cinderella	Puss-in-Boots
Blue Beard	dragon
Giant	Fairy Godmother

GROUP SECRETS

This game can also be played in groups. Half the class act as a panel and the other half agree to the name of a book character, say, Huckleberry Finn. The panel has five minutes to guess the character. Children answer yes or no to make sure the questions are carefully thought through.

CARTOONS

Students can bring cartoon strips to school. Select a few cartoons and white out the words in the bubbles. Enlarge the cartoons by using an overhead projector. Ask children to suggest dialogue for each bubble. A comic story usually has a frame to set the scene, the next develops the plot, the next contains the main action or climax, and the final frame is the conclusion. This can be done as a class activity, or individual students may devise their own dialogue. As well as learning about simple plot structure, children have to use words concisely and build up effective punchlines.

DEVISE YOUR OWN CHOOSE-YOUR-ADVENTURE BOOKS

Begin with a setting and at least two characters. Write up an opening paragraph on the board or a large chart:

> The aliens were restless. They had been circling the earth for several months now. Suddenly a blinding flash of light took them by surprise. Next minute they were

> **A**
> hurtling off into deepest space

> **B**
> hurtling towards earth

Children then split into two groups to write a paragraph for A and another for B. At the conclusion of the next paragraph another decision A or B has to be made and the group divides again. So the sequence goes on until each child is left to make individual conclusions. The choose-your-own adventure can be typed up, illustrated and placed in the library.

TIME-LINE CHART

Make a time-line chart of a character's life taken from a favorite book. Begin the time line as you begin the story and fill in events as the story proceeds.

CHARACTER ROLL OUT

This activity is based on the game Dungeons and Dragons. Children need two dice and a list of character elements. Some beginning character elements are listed, but it is more effective if the children invent their own.

Children roll the dice first of all to decide on the character's occupation. Then they roll of the dice for appearance, and so on.

	Occupation		Appearance
1	warrior	1	overweight
2	thief	2	tall
3	lawyer	3	sickly
4	doctor	4	intelligent
5	schoolteacher	5	thin
6	child	6	slow
7	counterfeiter	7	robust
8	film star	8	dull
9	hobo	9	short
10	pilot	10	elderly
11	politician	11	active
12	rock star	12	youthful

Past experiences	Main goal
1 soldier of fortune	1 to gather riches
2 prisoner	2 to provide for the poor
3 hospitalized	3 healthy life
4 developed ESP	4 happy life
5 special strength	5 power and glory
6 eternal youth	6 save the world from danger
7 computerized brain	
8 from a happy family	
9 alien	
10 reincarnated	
11 normal life developed	
12 special X-Ray vision	

Once a character has been created children may invent stories based on that character. Several characters may be invented and they may be used in group stories.

PLOT WHEEL OR STORY WHEEL

Spin the wheel and choose the story genre, event, setting, and up to three characters.

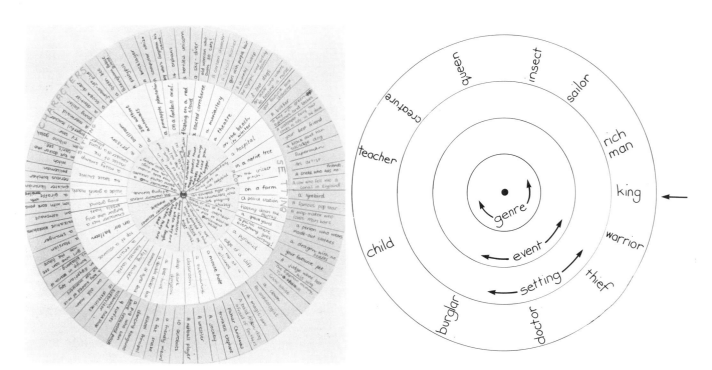

A plot wheel developed together by children and the teacher.

Alternatively, place the words on cards in boxes and select. The following example has some suggestions:

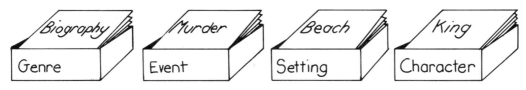

Genre	**Event**	**Setting**	**Character**
Biography	Kidnapping	The Beach	(Select up to three)
Science Fiction	Murder	Mountains	King Sailor
Mystery	Lost at Sea	Underground	Warrior Rich Man
Historical Fiction	A Battle	On Water	Thief Rich Woman
Fantasy	Held for Ransom	High Place	Doctor Poor Man
School Stories	Smuggling	Desert	Lawyer Poor Woman
Adventure	Lost Jewels	City	Child Police Officer
Poetry	A Set-up	Different	Teacher
Animal Story	Spying	Land	Creature
Comedy	Mistaken Identity	The Country	Queen
		The Tropics	Insect

GENRE SELECTION

Make charts of the different kinds of literature and have them displayed in the school.

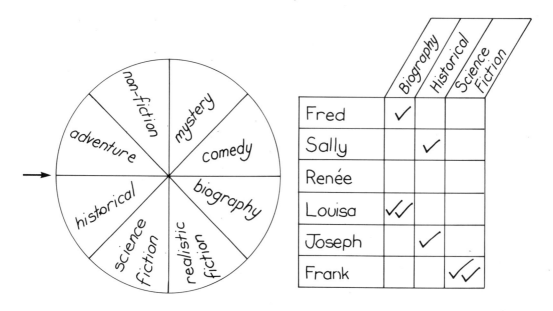

Spin the wheel and choose a different kind of book today. A chart nearby would record children's reading. Each time children read a book from a different genre they place a tick in the box.

PLOT PARAGRAPHS

Practice telling someone in the class the plot of a story until children can get the plot down to three or four sentences or one paragraph.

WORKING WITH LITERARY MOTIFS

What do these literary motifs signify?

wolf	lion	lamb
cupid	blossoming	old age
vulture	trees	fire
serpent	dragons	jewels
shepherd	angel	birds flying
forest	sword	thunder
flowers	ice and snow	

COLOR AND SEASON SYMBOLS

What do various seasons signify in stories? What about various colors, for example black or white and silver or red? Brainstorm characters associated with colors, for example:

White	**Black**	**Red**
white knight	black knight	Little Red Riding
angels	devils	Hood
good cowboys	bad cowboys	
wearing white hats	wearing black hats	
white doves	spiders	
Snow White	Black Queen	

ROULETTE STORIES

One person begins the story and passes it to another person in a small group. As the story is passed around, the group children have to keep characters consistent and develop a believable plot with a beginning, a middle, and an end.

CHARACTER RATING SCALE

Children may rate a character along a five-point continuum. Children place an *X* or a cutout circle or spot in the most appropriate space. This activity can be successfully developed for a large group, small group or as an individual activity (O'Sullivan 1984).

Rating Scale: Character's Name: WOLF					
	very	quite	neither	quite	very
good				✓		bad
independent	✓					dependant
brave				✓		coward
hot		✓				cold
honest				✓		dishonest
strong	✓					weak
kind				✓		cruel
happy			✓			sad

THE GREAT BOOKS

6

The rationale for using this approach in the classroom is the importance of presenting children with the best quality literature or literature that has stood the test of time and still remains popular. Many people claim that particular books—the classics—have great cultural importance because they transmit the important values of a culture. Leavis (1969) states that good literature forms a heritage and that reading, absorbing, and imitating that heritage imparts cultural values to the young. So not only does the great books approach stress the importance of presenting the classics of the particular culture to children because of their merit or literary quality, but often the values inherent in the great books are to be fostered in some way in the mind of the reader.

The great books or classics

These include books that have stood the test of time and remained popular such as *Alice in Wonderland* or the fairytale *Cinderella* and the award winners from English-speaking countries in other parts of the world. Most countries have awards for books considered to be of great literary merit. In the United States the Caldecott Medal is awarded to the best picture book and the Newbery Medal to the best novel. In Canada, The Canadian Library Award and Amelia Frances Gibbon Award are awarded, respectively, to the best children's book and best-illustrated children's book. In the United Kingdom the picture book award is known as the Kate Greenaway Medal and the novel is awarded the Carnegie Medal. Australian awards for best picture book and novel are also presented each year. Lists of these award winners are found in Appendix III (pages 125–137).

CULTURAL CLASSICS

Each country has books considered classics within its culture. Canadian classics include *Anne of Green Gables* by Lucy Maud Montgomery and Roch Carrier's *The Hockey Sweater*. *Little House on the Prairie* by Laura Ingalls Wilder, and *Tom Sawyer* and *Huckleberry Finn* by Mark Twain are well-known American classics. Possibly teachers and children have other favorites and these titles may be just the beginning of a list to be compiled in the classroom.

BEGINNING WITH THE GREAT BOOKS

For very young children, employing the great books approach would entail first listening to nursery rhymes, folk tales, and fairytales. Some of the nursery rhymes we all know as part of our culture were originally adult rhymes and are seen as important for children to know. For example, *A Frog He Would a Wooing Go* is a satiric rhyme about forty-nine-year-old Queen Elizabeth I who was wooed by a twenty-three-year-old French prince, and Humpty Dumpty is about the death of Richard III. *Punch and Judy* was originally about Punch (England) and Judy (France) as they fought over Italy, and *Sing a Song of Sixpence* was devised to make comment on the marriages of Henry VIII. (For more explanations of the origins of nursery rhymes, see Norton, 1983, pages 173-174.)

The great books approach would also include fairytales, folk tales, legends, and some myths in the early years. Many of these tales have been handed down verbally from generation to generation.

FOLK TALES

These are prose narratives that are regarded as fiction and are not really taken seriously. Folk tales usually tell of the adventures of animal or human characters who often meet with supernatural adversaries such as ogres, witches, giants, and terrible beasts. Some folk tales may be cumulative like *Henny Penny* and *The Gingerbread Boy*, where the tale repeats various phrases and actions. Some are humorous such as *The Tale of the Turnip*. Others are beast tales such as *The Three Billy Goats Gruff*. Some folk tales are knows as *pourquoi* tales which answer a question such as "Why the rabbit has a short tail" or "Why the spider spins a web." (See page 78.)

FAIRYTALES

These tales contain an element of magic: fairy godmother, frogs who change to princes, fairies, and witches. Good and bad magic may exist. When bad magic is performed, diligence, hard work, love, and goodness usually overcome it. *Snow White and the Seven Dwarfs, Cinderella, Jack and the Beanstalk* are examples of fairytales. Good collections of fairytales were made by Charles Perrault and the Brothers Grimm.

LEGENDS

Legends are prose narratives regarded as true by the narrator but set in a remote time and place. For example, the legends of King Arthur and Robin Hood are considered to have their roots in fact.

MYTHS

Myths are often considered as truthful accounts of what happened in the remote past. They account for natural phenomena such as the origin of the world, death and birth. The Greek myths tell of the gods and goddesses on Olympus who were involved in creating day and night, the seasons, war and peace.

Greek and Roman gods

Greek	Roman	
Zeus	Jupiter	Symbolizes King of Gods and people
Athena	Minerva	Goddess of Wisdom
Aphrodite	Venus	Goddess of Love and Beauty
Apollo	Apollo	God of Sun
Eros	Cupid	God of Love
Ares	Mars	God of War
Artemis	Diana	Goddess of the Moon
Demeter	Ceres	Goddess of Crops
Hermes	Mercury	Messenger of the Gods
Poseidon	Neptune	God of the Sea and Earthquakes
Hephaestus	Vulcan	God of Fire
Dionysius	Bacchus	God of Wine and Drama

POURQUOI STORIES

Pourquoi (meaning "why" in French) tales were written to answer questions about why animals act in certain ways or look as they do. Children may listen to *pourquoi* stories such as *Why the Crab Has a Hard Back* and write their own such as *Why the Chicken Cannot Fly*, *Why a Flea Jumps*, *Why Dogs Have Fur*, *Why Koalas Live in Trees*.

FABLES

Fables are moral tales in which animals act as humans, for example *The Hare and the Tortoise*. The moral of this fable is that perseverance and determination compensate for the lack of other attributes.

Classics or award winners

The following books can be considered as books not to be missed in the classroom.

K–2 LOWER PRIMARY, TEN OF THE BEST

Ahlberg, Janet and Ahlberg, Allen. *Each Peach Pear Plum*, Kestrel, Harmondsworth, 1978.

Allen, Pamela. *Who Sank the Boat?* Hamish Hamilton, London, 1982.

Bemelmans, Ludwig. *Madeline*. Viking, New York, 1977.

Burningham, John. *Mr Gumpy's Outing*. Cape, London, 1970.

Emberley, Barbara. *Drummer Hoff*. Prentice-Hall, Englewood Cliffs, New Jersey, 1967.

Fox, Mem. *Possum Magic*, illustrated by Julie Vivas. Harcourt Brace Jovanovich, San Diego, 1990.

Gag, Wanda. *Millions of Cats*. Faber, London, 1928.

Hutchins, Pat. *Rosie's Walk*. Macmillan, New York, 1968.

Sendak, Maurice. *Where the Wild Things Are*. Harper, New York, 1963.

Van Allsburg, Chris. *Jumanji*. Houghton Mifflin, Boston, 1981.

3–4 THE MIDDLE YEARS, TEN OF THE BEST

Bierhost, John (trans.). *The Glass Slipper: Charles Perrault's Tales of Times Past*. Four Winds Press, Bristol, Florida, 1981.

Cleary, Beverly. *Ramona the Pest*. William Morrow, New York, 1974.

Coerr, Eleanor. *Sadako and the Thousand Paper Cranes*. Putnam, New York, 1977.

Dahl, Roald. *Revolting Rhymes*, illustrated by Quentin Blake. Cape, London, 1982.

Hughes, Ted. *The Iron Man: A Story in Five Nights*. Faber, London, 1985.

Lamorisse, Albert. *The Red Balloon*. Doubleday, New York, 1978.

Lewis, C.S. *The Lion, the Witch and the Wardrobe*. Macmillan, New York, 1983.

Wagner, Jenny. *The Nimbin*. Thomas Nelson, Melbourne, 1978.

White, E.B. *Charlotte's Web*. HarperCollins, New York, 1973.

4–7 UPPER PRIMARY, TEN OF THE BEST

Byars, Betsy. *The Pinballs*. HarperCollins, New York, 1977.

Cooper, Susan. *The Dark is Rising*. Atheneum, New York, 1976.

French, Simon. *Cannily Cannily*. Angus and Robertson, Sydney, 1981.

Kelleher, Victor. *Master of the Grove*. Kestrel, Harmondsworth, 1982.

Park, Ruth. *Playing Beatie Bow*. Puffin, Harmondsworth, 1982.

Paterson, Katherine. *Bridge to Terabithia*. HarperCollins, New York, 1980.

Pearce, Philippa. *Tom's Midnight Garden*. Lippincott, Philadelphia, 1958.

Tolkien, J.R.R. *The Hobbit*. Unwin, London, 1987.

Westall, Robert. *The Machine Gunners*. NY: Greenwillow, 1976.

Wrightson, Patricia. *The Nargun and the Stars*. NY: Atheneum, 1974.

Ways of working with the great books

➺ Read two or three versions of a fairytale or folk tale such as *Sleeping Beauty, Little Red Riding Hood, Cinderella, Peter and the Wolf* or *The Nightingale* by Hans Christian Andersen. After reading both versions encourage children to discuss the illustrations, the characters, scenery, colors, details, and actions. Make a list on a chart where children note similarities and differences.

Cinderella 1	**Cinderella 2**	**Cinderella 3**
Fairy godmother as an old woman.	Fairy godmother as a witch.	Fairy godmother as a fairy.
Stepsisters unnamed.	Stepsisters named Charlotte and Euphronia.	Stepsisters unnamed.

John Warren Stewig (1984) suggests that children discuss the similarities and differences between books with the same title. Younger children dictate these differences while older children write their own responses. Whether writing or dictating students learn to use words to describe what they see and read and to make comparisons.

➡ Rewrite a classic but set it in the present. For example, write a modern day fairytale or legend or a modern version of a classic such as *Gulliver's Travels*. Perhaps write a regional version of *Wind in the Willows*, *Alice in Wonderland*, or *Treasure Island*.

➡ Find out which books are the most popular in your own library and make a list. (Look at the library cards to find out the most frequently borrowed.)

➡ Keep records of the most popular book in the classroom.

➡ Develop your own classroom classics or best-loved stories. Share them with others in the class and keep track of how many books are read by individual children. (Remember some children read quickly and some read slowly. One long classic could take a year to read.)

➡ Have a fairytale festival where favorite characters are illustrated or perhaps made into portraits for visitors to guess their names. Combine this with storytelling of favorite fairytales, a play made up from a fairytale or a modern version of a traditional tale. This festival may be combined with a Christmas or a mid-year festival.

➡ Children in upper primary grades assume the character of their favorite mythical character and write in autobiographical style to tell the story of the character's life.

➡ Discuss common elements in fairytales, such as extremely good and extremely bad characters. Talk about these characters in the stories read in class and make a list of them from fairytales.

Good characters	Bad characters
pigs	wolf
Little Red Riding Hood	wolf
Snow White	stepmother/witch
Jack	Giant

➡ Cut up old versions of fairytale books and glue pages to a card. Children can sequence the stories or change them in some way. Mixing up fairytales can be fun.

➡ Make big books of fairytales. Invite children to complete the moral at the end of the fairytales. For example, they may complete the moral or morals to *Little Red Riding Hood* by saying:

"Don't talk to wolves."
"Don't disobey your parents."
"Don't walk through a forest by yourself" and so on.

➡ Find the old version of a particular fairytale and set up a display. It is possible to find many versions of *Cinderella* and also to show how the illustrations have changed over time.

➡ Children may want to write their own versions of fairytales.

➡ Read selections of picture books. Include some award winners and non-award winners and ask children to list their favorites. Discuss their reasons for wanting to hear particular stories several times. Why do some stories become favorites?

➡ Discuss whether fairytales are sexist. Are females always portrayed as passive, diligent, and obedient and males always strong, courageous, and intelligent?

➡ Read a selection of award winners over a school term. Children may write class reviews on large charts.

➡ Rewrite a classic in cartoon form. Make sure the basic plot stays the same and the cartoon is set in the same period as the story.

➡ Make a plot board game. Take a well-known story such as *Treasure Island*. Children then develop a board game where players roll dice in order to move through the sequence of the plot, for example:

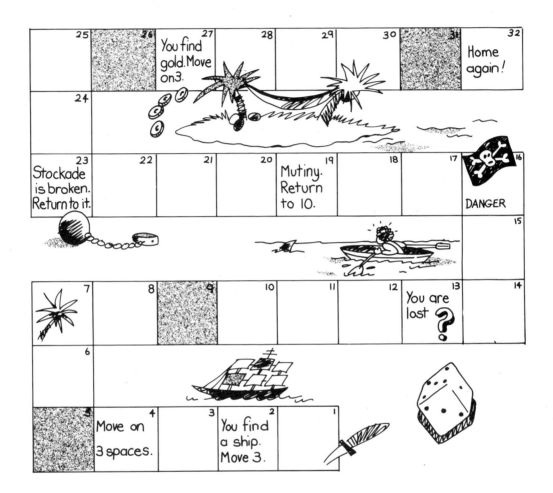

Or a snakes and ladders game based on Charlotte's Web.

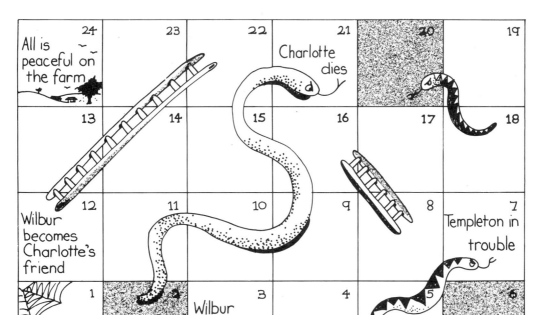

➤ Convert some folk tales or fairytales into reader's theater and perform these at school assemblies.

➤ Make glove puppets, sock puppets, or shadow puppets to dramatize folk tales. Sometimes the folk tale can be modified; sometimes new tales, such as *pourquoi* tales, can be invented.

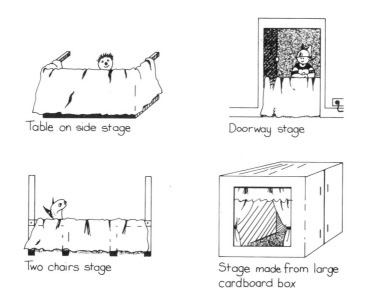

Table on side stage

Doorway stage

Two chairs stage

Stage made from large cardboard box

➡ Make a collection of folk tales from all over the world. Show on a world map where they originated.

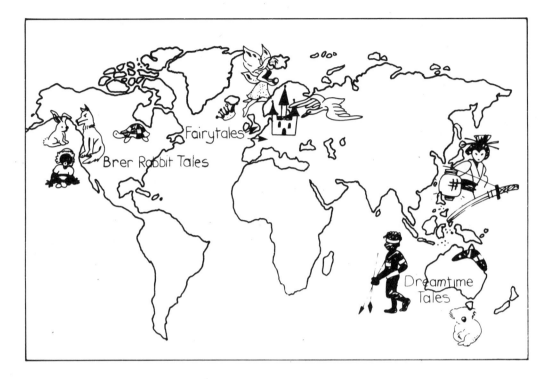

LITERATURE-BASED READING PROGRAMS

Many teachers use four approaches to literature-based reading by sometimes focusing on the **author**, at other times the **story**, children's **response**, and the **classic** tales. Recently critical literacy has shown great possibilities for exploring power and the portrayal of gender, race, and class in literature (Comber 1993). Teachers now examine how power, point of view, and ways different views of the world are constructed in books. The persuasive power of story and point of view is acknowledged in literature-based reading programs.

Children are shaped by literature as through their imagination they are drawn into the story and sometimes feel compassion and anger, laughter, joy, and at times exasperation at the injustice experienced by characters in books. As a child I was shaped by the story of *The Three Little Pigs*, which stressed hard work and delayed gratification. The moral of this tale is don't build your house out of straw or the wolf will get you. Only recently I have questioned why the pigs worked individually and didn't collaborate to build a great house together—and why we continue to stereotype wolves as villains.

Literature and celebrating diversity

Literature encourages children to view the world from another's eyes, to explore voice and perspective-taking so that different worlds can be understood and appreciated. Through literature children can explore problem solving and ways characters deal with conflict within self, conflict between self and group, and conflict between self and society. Children can also explore issues to do with equity, diversity, and justice.

Literature is about

- ▶ feelings and imagination
- ▶ exploring words and images that awaken senses
- ▶ hearing the world from another's voice
- ▶ confronting our values when faced with conflict
- ▶ exploring issues to do with diversity and justice

USING TEACHING STRATEGIES THAT ENCOURAGE DIVERSITY AND PARTICIPATION

Literature is a way to increase children's social consciousness; this means not just repeating the traditional powerful teacher role but using strategies so that student's voices are heard and power is shared in the classroom. Instead of the teacher being the sole arbitrator of how to interpret or respond to a text, she invites diversity, debate, and different points of view by using cooperative learning strategies.

To build a classroom community of supportive learners, cooperative strategies are used to encourage students to critique each other's ideas, to engage in discussions of controversial issues, and to maintain positive peer relationships. Cooperative learning structures, like partner work and group jigsaws, are used to improve classroom interactions and to increase participation of all students. The power and status of previously dominant individuals are made explicit and the class has self awareness about its group interaction skills. The traditionally invisible curriculum of peer interactions is made visible.

The class works in heterogeneous groups to break down cliques and increase the range of ideas and opinions. Working productively with others in groups is not an innate ability; it is learned. Many teachers explicitly teach turn taking, ways to criticize ideas and not people, ways to play different group roles, and strategies to use to reach decisions and consensus. By using cooperative learning, the students monitor how they work, who does particular tasks, and who makes decisions.

The following literature-based program is a collaborative effort between myself, a university teacher in language and literacy courses, and Jane O'Loughlin, a teacher of eleven- and twelve-year-old children in an independent school in Adelaide, Australia. We have found working together in the classroom, trying new ideas, and challenging existing practices is intellectually stimulating. We read books with the class, try new ways to explore texts, and both of us bring new ideas, a new perspective, different views and challenges, which enrich our teaching. These fundamental ideas of inviting diversity and seeking different points of view occur in Jane's literature program.

Jane's literature-based program

There are three components to Jane's literature-based program. **Read Aloud** is when Jane reads to the whole class. **Literature Group** is when heterogeneous groups of children read a book over four to five weeks and meet with the teacher to discuss their reading. **Book Conference** is when Jane meets a student to discuss books read individually.

READ ALOUD

There are times in Read Aloud when Jane focuses on an **author**, for example, reading books by Katherine Paterson. They explore the author's craft and the themes the author wants the reader to explore and understand, like sibling rivalry, the strength of childhood friendship, death, and renewal.

There are times when the genre or structure of the **story**, setting and use of different characters are a focus. Sometimes Jane reads a selection from the great **classics** and traditional tales; sometimes picture books, short stories and award-winning classics are selected. Literary merit is important in selecting these books as the best examples of author craft, story, themes and issues are chosen as a focus for the whole class.

In Read Aloud Jane reads books the students would not necessarily choose for themselves. Picture books or sections of novels like *The Chocolate War* by Robert Cormier and Charles Dickens' *A Christmas Carol* are placed side by side to explore the theme of greed. Sometimes Read Aloud becomes a demonstration of a particular author's craft of imagery, plot, or character development.

At times, social issues within the classroom are a stimulus for Jane choosing particular books. For example a child in the class was being victimized and called "fatty" so Jane read a piece from *Blubber* by Judy Blume; the class then discussed the social construction of "fatness." As Sapon-Shevin (1993) suggests, children can discuss how "some people decide what women's bodies should look like and perpetuate that image through the media and advertising…[how] we are all hurt by narrow rigid ways of looking at difference."

Jane may at times select several books to explore issues like gender stereotyping. She reads *A Job for Wittilda* by Caralyn and Mark Buehner and *My Wicked Stepmother* by Norman Leach to explore stereotyping and ageism of women, witches, and stepmothers. She reads *Piggybook* by Anthony Browne and *Mum Goes to Work* by Libby Gleeson to explore gender stereotyping of mothers in picture books.

Jane is fascinated with how point of view affects the story and what is left out or included in a story. She has collected books that demonstrate different points of view. Sometimes there are two stories in the same book like *The Pain and the Great One* by Judy Blume. Sometimes there are two points of view running parallel in a book like *Come Away from the Water, Shirley* by John Burningham or *Kirsty Knows Best* by Analena McAfee. Sometimes Jane reads stories told by characters who have not told their story, like *The True Story of the Three Little Pigs* by Jon Scieszka (where the wolf's version of the story is told). She has also read *The Stinky Cheeseman and Other Fairly Stupid Tales* by Scieszka to explore alternative versions of the traditional tales.

Books are read aloud to

➡ introduce an author, genre, or aspect of story
➡ explore different responses to a story
➡ introduce classic tales and award-winning books
➡ counter sexist, ageist, racist stereotyping
➡ explore whose voice tells the story
➡ increase social consciousness about themes to do with power, relationships, and conflict

LITERATURE GROUP

The Literature Group part of the program involves four to six members in heterogeneous groups. In the class there are five literature groups. Each group reads a different book. Sometimes the whole class reads one book but they discuss the books in Literature Group.

Each Literature Group meets weekly to discuss the book, usually proceeding a few chapters at a time. During one ten-week term the groups used the following cooperative structures:

> mind maps
> mini-jigsaw
> literature roulette
> judge the book
> partner scripts
> blooming questions
> QAPX

Mind Maps

The group reads several chapters in a book, for example, *Onion Tears*, the story of an Asian boat child, by Diana Kidd. The group takes one large sheet of paper and a colored marker for each group member. The group chooses a topic from those listed on the chalkboard:

> **Issues to discuss**
> peace
> conflict
> differences
> relationships
> problem
> prejudice
> justice
> oppression

Today the group chose peace and made a mind map to do with peace. A mind map is a drawing or series of drawings, a diagram, or a picture illustrating the elements and relationships associated with a particular idea.

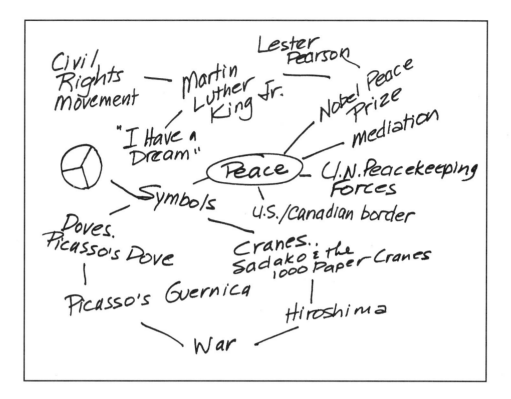

The group has about thirty minutes to plan and create a mind map. As each person has a different colored pen, individual accountability is built into the cooperative group activity.

Mini-Jigsaw

In mini-jigsaw each person in the group takes an aspect of the story to research and provides information to the group. Each individual student selects one of the following cards:

AUTHOR BIOGRAPHY CARD

Find and list ten facts about this author's background.

CHARACTER CARD

How is the setting important to the character? Draw the main character or main characters and list vocabulary to describe them.

PLOT CARD

List the conflicts so far. What choices do the characters have? Predict what will happen next.

SETTING CARD

Illustrate the setting. Research information about the setting by using a world atlas, street directories, or other geographical reference books.

AUTHOR'S CRAFT

Find three examples of how the author uses imagery, figurative language, or word play to get the reader into the story.

When all the information is completed the group compiles a poster on chart paper inviting others to read the book. The poster can have these sections: author biography, characters, plot, setting, and author craft.

Literature Roulette

The questions are generic and suit any book. They are written on a small roulette wheel. Children prepare answers and reasons for their answers to each question on the roulette wheel before they meet in literature group. The roulette wheel can be spun or alternatively dice can be thrown and children take turns answering.

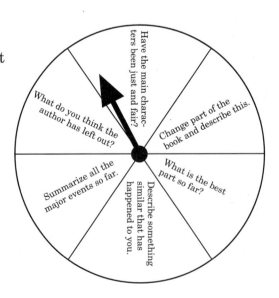

Judge the Book

Judge the Book helps children identify the relationships between actions of the characters and the values they hold, and develops strategies to analyze characters in books. The activity also encourages the reader to interpret different motives and points of view of the characters. The skills of careful listening and questioning are practiced.

To begin divide the class into randomly selected groups of six. Within each group, assign the following roles:

> **Judge**: Keeps order, asks for clarification, decides with the jury's help who is guilty and who is not.
> **Defense**: Presents a case to defend the accused.
> **Prosecutor**: Presents a case to convict the accused.
> **Accused**: Is accused of the crime. Must answer questions asked by the prosecutor and the defender.
> **Two Witnesses**: Can be any character who can add insight into the case. Give their points of view in response to questions from the prosecutor or defense.

When introducing Judge the Book to the students, Jane asks the whole class to prepare the first trial. She uses a novel she is reading aloud to demonstrate the process. For example, in *The Lion, the Witch and the Wardrobe* by C.S Lewis, Edmund is accused of lying about Narnia. Alternatively Jane could use a literature-group book such as *The Chocolate War*, where Archie is accused of using psychological intimidation.

Jane assigns groups of six and divides each group in half. Three students develop a case for the defense and three students develop a case for the prosecution.

Witnesses may be selected from the other characters in the novel. Both the defense and the prosecution should select witnesses who will support their interpretation of the argument. The role of the witness is to answer questions according to that character's point of view. It is useful to provide the students with questions to guide their preparation and scripts to guide their presentation of the case.

Guide questions

What is your point of view?
What evidence can you provide from the text to support your point of view?
What do you think the opposing point of view will be?
How can you refute this argument?

JUDGE: Today we will hear the case against _____ from
the novel _____.
_____ is accused of _____.
Acting for the defense is _____.
Acting for the prosecution is _____.
Will the prosecutor call their first witness?

PROSECUTOR: I call _____.
Please state your name and your relationship to the accused.

WITNESS: I am _____ and my relationship to
_____ is _____.

PROSECUTOR: [*Asks the witness questions. When finished says…*]
No more questions Your Honor.

JUDGE: The defense may cross-examine.

DEFENSE: [*Asks questions to try to rebut the witness's evidence. When finished
says…*].
No more questions Your Honour.

JUDGE: The defense may call their witness

DEFENSE: I call _____.

Please state your name and your relationship to the accused.

WITNESS: I am _____ and my relationship to
_____ is _____.

DEFENSE: [*Asks the witness questions. When finished says…*]
No more questions Your Honor.

JUDGE: The prosecutor may call the accused.

PROSECUTOR: [*May ask questions.*]

DEFENSE: [*Can cross-examine. When finished says…*]
No more questions Your Honor.

JUDGE: The jury must now make their decision.
Who finds the accused guilty of _____?
[*Counts the votes.*]
Who find the accused innocent of _____?
[*Counts the votes.*]
In the trial of _____ I find the accused
[guilty/not guilty] of _____.

The court is now dismissed.

Script for presentation of the case.

After the trial students can discuss the evidence used to support the case. Did the evidence change your opinion of the characters? What do you think the author thought about the character? Did the questions encourage the witnesses to give relevant information? Is there any way the trial could be improved for next time?

Partner Scripts

Groups of four or six split into pairs to work with people they do not usually work with. Partners assign themselves A or B. The pairs negotiate how much they will read before discussing the text. Partner A reads a paragraph, page, or several pages of a novel. Then the text is covered. Partner B summarizes what has been read. Partner A checks for key ideas left out. Both then create a metaphor or analogy to help remember the information. Partner B reads the next paragraph, then puts the text out of sight while Partner A summarizes and so on. The collaborative learning script is for partners to work together to understand texts. Jane finds that the collaborative learning script works with nonfiction and fiction.

1. Flip a coin to see who will be Partner A and Partner B.
2. Each partner reads passage one.
3. When finished they put the passage out of sight.
4. Partner A orally summarizes the contents of passage one.
5. Partner B detects and corrects any errors in Partner A's summary (metacognitive step).
6. Both partners work together to develop analogies, images, metaphors to help make the summarized information memorable.
7. Each partner reads passage two.
8. Repeat steps 4–6 with partners reversing roles.
   (based on Dansereau 1986)

Blooming Questions [1]

Generic questions are placed on cards (see page 94) and the group comes to the discussion group prepared to answer three questions. Cards are turned down and randomly picked up by the group as they take turns around the circle. Group members listen to add information or ideas not provided by classmates.

---

1. This activity is based on the work of Bloom (1956) and Kagan (1980).

KNOWLEDGE

List the events so far in sequential order.

UNDERSTANDING

List three choices the character had. Why were some decisions made and not others?

ANALYSIS

Find examples of self/self conflict, self/group conflict, self/society conflict. Describe these for the group.

APPLICATION

Discuss a similar experience you have had. How was it similar? What made it different?

EVALUATION

What is the author's message? Does it help you understand why some characters and behavior are valued and others are not? Does it try to build a better world? Is the book successful? Why? Why not?

SYNTHESIS

Change a character and tell what would happen next. Change part of the plot and tell what could happen.

QAPX

This is a cooperative question-and-answer activity suitable for any book or part of book.

In groups of four (if there are six then have three people provide extra information):

Q: Person 1 asks a question about the reading.

A: Person 2 provides an answer.

P: Person 3 paraphrases the answer by framing it in a new way.

X: Person 4 provides extra information not given in the answers.

The group rotates with person 2 asking a question, then person 3, and so on.

Jane has a literature group meet each day of the week so that she can sit in and join the discussion. She also keeps notes for assessment and challenges the group to look from different viewpoints or to provide more information.

INDIVIDUAL READING

Children read independently, often reading books of their choice but also books selected with Jane's guidance. The children organize a book conference every two weeks by writing their names on a chart on the day they will be ready to discuss the completed book.

Organizing times for book conferences.

To prepare for a book conference the children select two questions from the following list. They must include one question from numbers 1–3 and one from numbers 4–6. They record their answers to the questions in the literature journals.

1. **Recall of information**
   Retell events
   Retell setting

Retell character description
Retell problem or conflict

2. **Reading between the lines**
   Why was this setting used?
   Why did the author choose these events and not others?
   How could the problem be seen differently?

3. **Applying ideas to own experiences**
   Have you had a similar experience?
   What would you do if this happened to you?
   What are different about your experiences and the characters?

4. **Analysis of elements within the narrative**
   Whose point of view is this?
   What other voices could tell the story?
   What effect does this character have on the plot?
   Who else could be in the story?

5. **Synthesis of ideas**
   Create a rap or chant about this story.
   Change the ending.
   Change an element within the story.

6. **Critical evaluation**
   Was this well written and believable?
   Is the message to create a better world?
   What was left out and why?
   Is this story right, just, or fair?

ASSESSMENT OF COOPERATIVE SKILLS IN LITERATURE GROUP

Assessment involves the development of reading and understanding of literature and of how the group works together. To assess cooperative skills the group selects a skill to focus on. The cooperative skill may have to do with communication: listening, turn taking, encouraging others, or working as a group; or playing group roles: encourager, recorder, challenger, time keeper, or organizer (Hill and Hill 1990; Hill and Hancock 1993). In problem solving the group may need to watch that they criticize ideas and not people, how they piggyback on other's ideas, ways they brainstorm, and how they define what the problem is.

The group selects one of the following skills to monitor as they work. Jane also observes for the use of these skills and gives feedback.

Communicating
listening
turn taking
encouraging others
no put downs

Problem solving
criticizing ideas not people
piggybacking
brainstorming
defining the problem

Group roles
encourager
recorder
organizer
challenger
time keeper

Managing differences
perspective taking
negotiation
mediation
making decisions

We will focus on _____ .

ASSESSMENT OF READING

Assessment of the children's reading has to do with retelling knowledge or information from the narrative—what happened? how? who to? where? when did it occur? Reading and interpreting the text, applying ideas from the story to personal experiences, and analyzing the elements of the story are important. Synthesizing and changing parts of a story and critically analyzing the author's motives are monitored by Jane.

Jane uses the following to record children's reading development.

NAME _____ .

Personal:
- [ ] interpretation of character and events
- [ ] relating to own experience
- [ ] comparing self to other characters

Critical:
- [ ] author's purpose and motives
- [ ] author's decisions and choices
- [ ] analysis of the use of power in the plot
- [ ] analysis of relationships between characters
- [ ] construction of the reader

Technical:
- [ ] knowledge of details/information
- [ ] story structure
- [ ] genre
- [ ] spelling
- [ ] expression
- [ ] handwriting

Rita's literature mentor program

The literature mentor program was developed because Rita could not find time in her program for book conferences. Rita organizes her class so that the whole class reads individual books during three or four sessions in a week. The children read for twenty minutes then write for ten minutes. They may write about the plot, characters, ideas, thoughts, similar experiences, and so on. A literature mentor reads these responses and replies with a written comment. The literature mentor may be a parent, another teacher in the school, or older children in the school. He or she should comment on the book and on the reader's response, without being judgmental. Rita also encourages children to complete a literature activity once the book has been read.

A range of activities is displayed on a chart in the classroom.

Book activities

1. Make a comic strip of the plot
2. Illustrate the characters
3. Make a map of where the story took place
4. Make up an advertisement for the book
5. Design a new cover
6. Read your favorite parts on the tape-recorder
7. Listen to tapes of favorite stories
8. Script a short play
9. Be a character and write to the class
10. Write to a friend about the book

In order that children experience a range of activities, Rita has another chart where children list their names and the activities completed.

Name	Activity									
	1	2	3	4	5	6	7	8	9	10
Ben			●	●	●					
Fred			●			●		●		
Sally					●			●		
Jane						●				
Sarah								●	●	●
Andrew	●		●		●					
Luke		●	●						●	
Gia		●		●		●				
Barton		●	●	●						
Loc Now	●					●	●			

Rita reads to her class each day, and sets up literature quizzes based on authors, titles, and characters in various books. She has many charts where children list words they like from the various books they have read. As happens in many literature-based programs, Rita's class integrates writing, oral language, and drama with reading, always making language a lively experience.

Whole-class literature activities

Teachers work in many ways with literature-based reading. Some teachers work with small groups while other classes have individualized literature-based reading where each child reads a different book of his or her choice. At times a teacher may read aloud from a favorite book, for example, *Bridge to Terabithia* by Katherine Paterson. Whole class activities may then be developed around this book. In order to ensure that a range of activities are tackled, the teacher may develop a *Bridge to Terabithia* "contract." Children undertake the activities over two to four weeks and a total of twenty points means the contract is completed.

Name_____

Contract Checklist: Bridge to Terabithia by Katherine Paterson

Activity/Envelope Number and Activity Description	Individual or Group Members.	Points	Date of Competition
eg. Construct a diorama of Terabithia or your own fantasy world.	Group: Paul John, Kerry	2	17/5/86

I have been involved in the above activities

Signed _____

Activities may be displayed on a board in the classroom or kept in numbered envelopes. Some suggested activities for *Bridge to Terabithia*, as an example, follow.[2]

1. **Personal response** [3]
   We each wish to succeed at something; make a list of your abilities and limitations and compare with a friend. I[ndividual] 2 G[roup] 2

2. **Personal response**
   Should Jess have felt guilty about being the fastest runner after Leslie's death? Tell about one time you have felt guilty. Do this in a few short sentences or write a story. I–2 G–1

3. **Personal response**
   What is a friend? Who is your best friend? Write a letter to your friend and tell him/her why you value your friendship. I–2 G–2

4. **Personal response**
   How do you cope with fear today? Make a list of ways you could cope. I–2 G–1

5. **Personal response**
   What is a sibling? How do you get on with yours? Write a poem about a brother or sister. I–2 G–1

6. **Personal response**
   Do you have any fears? What are they? Write a story or poem about your fears. I–2 G–1

7. **Tape-recorder**
   1. Draw a picture from the book on an overhead.
   2. Write a script to accompany your picture.
   3. Tape-record the script.
   I–1 G–2

8. **Models**
   Construct a model of Terabithia or your own fantasy world. I–1 G–2

9. **Models**
   Make a corner of your classroom into your own fantasy world. What is its name? I–4 G–2

10. **Models**
    Make a corner of your classroom into the Terabithia created by Jess and Leslie. I–4 G–2

11. **Art**
    Design posters to advertise your own fantasy land. I–2 G–1

12. **Art**
    Design and create posters to advertise the book. I–2 G–1

13. **Art**
    Paint portraits of the main characters in the book. I–2 G–2

---

2. I am indebted to Trish Widera for these ideas.
3. Points are allocated for individual work or group work.

14. **Art**

Paint a mural of the Terabithia portrayed in the book. I–2 G–1

15. **Tape-recorder**

Tape-record some exciting passages from the book. I–2 G–1

16. **Discuss**

Relate the relationship of the two main characters to the one you have with a friend or a brother/sister. G–2

17. **Games**

Design and make a board game called My Own Terabithia. I–4 G–2

18. **Discuss**

How does the relationship between Jess and May Belle develop throughout the book? Show evidence in chapters of its growth. G–2

19. **Maths**

Draw a map of your fantasy land on graph paper and show its natural features using coordinates, e.g. there is a river at (6,9). I–2

20. **Other reading**

Try to find other books about fantasy lands (e.g. *Narnia* books by C.S. Lewis). How do these compare? I–2 G–1

21. **Written expression**

Design and make a passport that will allow you to travel from one land to another. I–2 G–1

22. **Other reading**

Find other books by Katherine Paterson. Display them. What is similar about them? I– 2 G–1

23. **Written expression**

Design and write a postcard to show the best features of your own fantasy land. I–2 G–1

24. **Drama**

Dramatize an exciting incident from the book. I– 2 G–1

25. **Discuss**

Are your own parents more like Jess's or Leslie's? Which family would you have preferred to belong to? G–2

26. **Other reading**

Try to find other books which explore the relationship between brothers and sisters (for example, *Welcome Home, Jellybean* by Marlene Fanta Shyer). Display them. I–2 G–1

27. **Discuss**

Why are friends important? G–2

28. **Drama**

Role-play an interview with the author of a book. G–1

There are many other kinds of contracts. Three examples follow.

1.

Reading Contract

I hereby do solemnly promise to complete this work
by _____

Signed _____   Signed _____
        (Student)   (Teacher)

Books:

1. _____
2. _____
3. _____
4. _____
5. _____
6. _____

Type of Material:

Tick the ones you have:

Fiction ◯
Non-fiction ◯
Story on tape ◯
Poetry ◯
Magazine ◯
Newspapers ◯
  eg. Kids Times
Other ◯ _____
_____

Activity:

I have decided to do this
activity _____
Book _____
Completed _____
              (Teacher Sign)

Conference:(Book Chat)
Date / / Sign _____
                        Teacher

Read Aloud:

I will read _____
to
Choose one
◯ Teacher
◯ Mum
◯ Dad
◯ Librarian
◯ Teacher aide
◯ Group of Yr 2 Children
◯ Other _____
_____

Signed _____
Comment : _____

Reporting:

In Reading Journal:
Book review   Yes/No
Comment and rating on
each book   Yes/No
Tch. Sign : _____

Shared:

I told _____ about
the book _____
Signed : _____
They liked the book Yes/No
They will read it   Yes/No
I told _____ about
the book _____
Signed : _____
They liked the book Yes/No
They will read it   Yes/No

Title of Book	Read Pages .... to .... (signed)	Rating /10	Discussed Book with	Book Chat with
		/10		
		/10		
		/10		
		/10		
		/10		
		/10		
		/10		

Novels, non-fiction poetry etc. variety encouraged.

2. –This was in the front of a cardboard book jacket. Children also had a Reading Journal.

3. –Children glue one of these in each page of their Reading Journals.

Book Title: ____________	Author: ____________
Book outline completed Signed ____________ (Teacher)	Oral reading: 2 pages read to ____________ Signed ____________
Activity selected ____________ Completed: Signed ____________ (Teacher)	Shared story with ____________ Signed ____________
Conference with teacher Date ________ Signed ________	Rating /10 9-10 Excellent 7-8 Good 5-6 Okay 1-4 Awful

Guided reading lesson

Many teachers encourage reading in small groups, say five or six children who are all reading the same book, at various times during the school year. At such times the guided reading lesson is an important strategy.

A literature group.

SELECTING THE TEXT

To begin the session, the teacher and the children select the text. It should not be too easy nor too difficult and must, of course, be relevant and interesting to the readers.

SELECTING A PURPOSE

Sometimes the purpose for reading will be to learn more about a new idea; at other times it may be enjoyment and discussion of the story read.

INTRODUCING THE STORY

When introducing the story, children are invited to predict what the story will be about, often basing their discussion on the title or illustrations. Children should have some strategies pointed out on how to deal with difficult words.

To discuss new concepts and new words, words may be written in a sentence on the blackboard so that children use the context of the sentence to predict the meaning and pronunciation of the word. If a particular word identification strategy is to be taught, for example the meaning of the prefix *un*, words containing this prefix should be listed on the blackboard by the teacher, then children invited to contribute other words containing the prefix. Reading text containing many new words will be more successful once most words are familiar.

In most cases, however, if the text does not contain many new words, children should be encouraged to read by gaining cues to the meaning of the new words from the context of the sentence. Too often time is spent teaching new words that children will have little difficulty with in proper context.

WHILE READING

Children read silently, and even the youngest readers are encouraged to read with their eyes in order to focus on the meaning.

AFTER READING

Children may retell parts of the story they liked best to the teacher or others in the group.

Shared books

Large books, either school made or commercially produced, enable small groups of children to share a story with the teacher. For beginning readers use of large print and a predictable structure in the form of repetitive syntax, for example:

> In the dark dark wood
> There was a dark dark house

is essential for building children's confidence in their ability to predict from the print cues. (See Appendix I for books with a predictable structure.)

There are three main stages in working with a big book (Holdaway 1979): initial sharing, rereading, and practice.

Initial sharing
Teacher reads the book to the children who join in when they have picked up the predictable structure.

Rereading
Here the teacher may draw children's attention to key words, particular concepts or ideas, word parts or phrases. A word frame can be used to isolate particular words for study.

Reading practice

Various oral reading strategies may be practiced, for example choral reading, paired reading, or teacher and children alternating reading.

Finally, of course, children respond and react to books by making new books, art work, drama, and by a range of activities from merely thinking about and reflecting on the story to mounting a large-scale dramatic production.

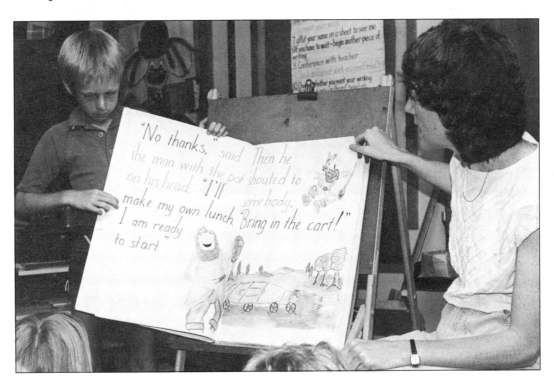

Big books made by the teacher or teacher's aide.

Matching children and text

If children are given opportunities to select the books they want to read they will develop into very discriminating text selectors. They will take account of the pictures, size of print, layout and topic or theme. The children may be encouraged to:

- ➠ look at the title to gauge the topic
- ➠ read the blurb on the front or back of the book
- ➠ flip through the book to look at the length
- ➠ talk to friends who may have read the book

Word-of-mouth recommendation from teachers and friends is a particularly strong factor in book selection (Hill 1984). If teachers watch out for interest-

Selecting books: A classroom check-out system for borrowing books from the class library.

ing books in the library and in bookshops, they can keep a wide range of books available to challenge the readers in their classes.

FIVE-FINGER TEST

Some teachers encourage children to try to read the first few pages of a book to see if it is suitable. For young children five fingers placed down for each unfamiliar word on the first page (or twenty words) of a book means that the book is too difficult. For older children five fingers placed down for difficult words in a fifty to one hundred word selection means that the book may be too difficult. However, it is always wise to try to read on through the first few pages as a book often gets easier to read once the basic ideas have been introduced.

CLOZE PROCEDURE

Some teachers develop cloze activities based on pages chosen from a literature group book. If a teacher deletes every fifth word from about 250 words of text and the child reads to 60 per cent accuracy, that is adding in appropriate words, the book is considered at the child's independent reading level (Kemp 1985). At 40 to 60 percent accuracy the book is considered instructional and below 40 per cent accuracy the book is definitely at the child's frustration level.

Small commercially published books can be made into big books to share in the classroom.

There was a robot I made from boxes.

Some of the teachers dressed up too.

My favourite story was George's Marvellous Medicine. The part I liked best was when everything grew LARGER.

Sheldon

A book review.

Puppet plays.

Ways of gathering information on children's responses to literature

Teachers are in a position to watch children carefully and note their responses to books. To gather an overview of classroom responses, Janet Hickman (1985) suggested keeping a log or journal. Here a teacher can jot down children's responses to one novel or their responses to individual books read. Journals can be used to jot down children's responses to thematic work, for example, the study of folk tales or fairytales.

CHILDREN'S JOURNALS OR DIARIES

If children keep a journal in a book or on a set of index cards and there is enough room for the teacher's response, then children's views of books read can be easily reviewed.

A teacher reflecting on the value of the reading program may ask these questions:

- ➼ What level of challenge do the children's choices represent?
- ➼ What are the preferred genres?
- ➼ Are there clusters of books by one author?
- ➼ What do the comments show about the students' implied criteria for a "good book"?
- ➼ What changes are reflected in the course of a year?

Keeping a response journal where a child and a teacher share ideas about books.

CHILDREN'S CLASSWORK BASED ON LITERATURE

Children may keep personal files of work, paintings, illustrations, charts of comparisons between books, and board games based on the plot of a book. For large dioramas, clay models, and murals, photographs can be taken and stored in the child's folder or file.

TAPE-RECORDINGS

Tape-recordings of individual book conferences or small group conferences provide a means of finding out more about children's views of books. Children's use of critical language, for example, words other than *good, nice,* or *OK,* their attitudes to various genres and to reading itself can be monitored. Such tape-recordings can be played to other teachers who may in turn offer new insights into the children's response. Pairs of children may sit down with a tape recorder and discuss books for the teacher to listen to later on in the busy day. Hickman (1985) states:

> The more sources that can be used in collecting evidence about children's interactions with books, poems and stories, the more helpful that evidence will be in guiding decisions on the selection and use of literature.

SUMMARY: THE MANY FORMS OF LITERATURE-BASED READING

A literature-based reading program not only provides rich content for the teaching of reading but helps also to extend children's imaginations and their understanding of the world by sharing in the world created by authors, while improving intellectual and affective growth. Literature acts as a model for children's writing, provides ideas for discussion involving listening and speaking, and extends children's understanding of language and ideas, all critical for further reading development.

Literature-based reading may consist of an individualized reading program where each child chooses and reads different books. Literature-based reading programs may also involve small group reading sessions that work in conjunction with individualized reading with teacher-student or peer book conferences. Some teachers beginning literature-based reading programs may read a favorite book to the class over a number of weeks with a variety of activities planned to encourage and extend children's responses to the story.

The focus of literature-based reading programs may vary. The teacher, following a child's lead, may help the child find out more about a particular **author** and the books written by that author. At other times, children may wish to respond in some way to the book read. This **response** may be to create a play, script, or a song based on the story. Perhaps writing, debating, art or craft work may be the medium for response. At other times, it may be appropriate to search out just what it is that makes up a **story**. In this approach, the various elements of story, style, and story genre may be explored. Other teachers planning a literature-based approach to the teaching of reading may incorporate the **great books** into the program. The classics—*Treasure Island*, *Charlotte's Web*, or *Alice in Wonderland* for example—may be read aloud or shared in literature groups. At various times during a year a class may focus on response, the author, the story, or the great books; or perhaps a teacher may combine aspects of all four in a literature-based program.

The many ideas that evolve from literature-based programs allow for rich interaction between the book, the child and peers, and between teacher and children. A class who has cried together over *Bridge to Terabithia* will know that emotions touch us in similar but different ways in a good story. A group who has decided to develop a melodrama from *Charlie and the Chocolate Factory* will discover each other's special talents, imagination, and diversity of responses to the story as they work together on producing a script.

Orchestrating a literature-based reading program requires a light hand. A teacher who overplans and overstructures a program misses the leads and directions the children may wish to take when responding to books. A heavy hand may result in repetitive book activities similar to those suggested by some basal reading programs. Overemphasis on literary theory and literary criticism will stifle the children's response and narrow their personal visions of what the story means to them.

A child creates meaning in life largely by using language, and this meaning is learned through social interaction (Vygotsky 1962). The role of the teacher is critical. The teacher must mediate between the child's world and the world of life and literature. For the teacher to see stories through children's eyes, to follow children's leads, and accompany and support them in particular quests as they search for meaning is the key to language exploration and reading development.

APPENDIX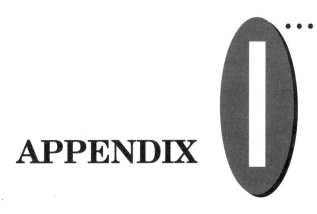

Books with predictable patterns

BOOKS WITH A REPETITIVE PATTERN

A certain phrase is repeated at various points.

Barrett, Judi. *Animals Should Definitely Not Wear Clothing*. New York: Atheneum, 1970.

Brown, Margaret Wise. *The Friendly Book*. New York: Golden Press, 1954.

Brown, Margaret Wise. *The Important Book*. New York: Harper and Row, 1949.

De Regniers, Beatrice Schenk. *May I Bring a Friend?* London: Methuen Children's Books, 1986.

Galdone, Paul. *The Little Red Hen*. New York: Clarion Books, 1973; Boston: Houghton Mifflin, 1973.

Galdone, Paul. *The Three Billy Goats Gruff*. New York: Seabury Press, 1973.

Joslin, Sesyle. *What Do You Say Dear?* New York: Scholastic Press, 1958.

Joyce, Irma. *Never Talk to Strangers*. New York: Golden Press, 1967.

Krauss, Ruth. *A Hole Is to Dig*. New York: Harper & Row, 1952.

Martin, Bill. *Brown Bear, Brown Bear, What Do You See?* New York: H. Holt, 1992.

Martin, Bill. *The Haunted House*. New York: Holt, Rinehart and Winston, 1970.

Paterson, A. B. *Waltzing Matilda*. New York: Holt, Rinehart and Winston, 1970.

BOOKS WITH A REPETITIVE-CUMULATIVE PATTERN

A word, phrase, or sentence is repeated in each succeeding episode, with each episode adding a new word, phrase, or sentence.

Berenstain, Stanley, and Janice Berenstain. *The B Book*. New York: Random House, 1971.

Bonne, Rose. *I Know an Old Lady*. New York: Scholastic Press, 1961.

Guilfoile, Elizabeth. *Nobody Listens to Andrew*. New York: Scholastic Press, 1957.

Mars, T. W. *The Old Woman and Her Pig*. Racine, WI: Western Publishing, 1964.

BOOKS WITH RHYMING PATTERNS

Many have rhyme combined with repetitions and cumulative-repetition.

Battaglia, Aurelius. *Old Mother Hubbard*. New York: Golden Press, 1972.

Brooke, Leslie. *Johnny Crow's Garden*. London: Frederick Warne and Co., 1968.

Cameron Polly. *I Can't Said the Ant*. New York: Coward, McCann, and Geoghegan, 1961.

Einsel, Walter. *Did You Ever See?* New York: Scholastic Press, 1962.

Emberley, Barbara. *Drummer Hoff*. Englewood Cliffs, NJ: Prentice-Hall, 1967.

Hoffman, Hilde. *The Green Grass Grows All Around*. New York: Macmillan, 1969.

Krauss, Ruth. *Bears*. New York: Scholastic Press, 1948.

Longstaff, John. *Frog Went A-Courting*. New York: Harcourt Brace Jovanovich, 1955.

Patrick, Gloria. *A Bug in a Jug*. New York: Scholastic Press, 1970.

Petersham, Maud, and Miska Petersham. *The Rooster Crows: A Book of American Rhymes and Jingles*. New York: Scholastic Press, 1971.

Watson, Clyde. *Father Fox's Pennyrhymes*. New York: Scholastic Press, 1971.

Withers, Carl. *A Rocket in My Pocket*. New York: Holt, 1988.

BOOKS WITH PATTERNS BASED ON FAMILIAR CULTURAL SEQUENCES

These include cardinal and ordinal numbers, alphabet, months of the year, days of the week, seasons, colors.

Cardinal and ordinal numbers

Alain. *One, Two, Three, Going to Sea*. New York: Scholastic Press, 1964.

Considine, Kate, and Ruby Schuler. *One, Two, Three, Four*. New York: Scholastic Press, 1965.

Emberley, Barbara, and Ed Emberley. *One Wide River to Cross*. New York: Scholastic Press, 1966.

Hoban, Tana. *Count and See*. New York: Macmillan, 1972.

Keats, Ezra Jack. *Over in the Meadow*. New York: Scholastic Press, 1971.

Martin, Bill. *A Ghost Story*. New York: Holt, Rinehart and Winston, 1970.

Palmer, Janet. *Ten Days of School*. Sydney, Australia: Macmillan, 1969.

Pavey, Peter. *One Dragon's Dream*. Melbourne, Australia: Thomas Nelson, 1979.

Quackenbush, Robert M. *Poems for Counting*. New York: Holt, Rinehart and Winston, 1965.

Alphabet

Baskin, Leonard. *Hosie's Alphabet*. New York: Viking, 1972.

Kraus, Robert. *Good Night Little ABC*. New York: Scholastic Press, 1972.

Memling, Carl. *Riddles, Riddles from A to Z*. New York: Golden Press, 1972.

Seuss, Dr. *Dr. Seuss's ABC*. New York: Random House, 1963.

Wildsmith, Brian. *Brian Wildsmith's ABC*. New York: Franklin Watts, 1962.

Days, months, and color

Martin, Bill. *Monday, Monday, I Like Monday*. Toronto: Holt, Rinehart and Winston, 1983.

O'Neill, Mary. *Hailstones and Halibut Bones*. New York: Doubleday, 1983.

Rossetti, Christine. *What Is Pink?* New York: Holt, Rinehart and Winston, 1965.

Sendak, Maurice. *Chicken Soup with Rice*. New York: Scholastic Press, 1962.

Wildsmith, Brian. *Twelve Days of Christmas*. New York: Franklin Watts, 1972.

Wright, H. R. *A Maker of Boxes*. New York: Holt, Rinehart and Winston, 1965.

BOOKS WITH PREDICTABLE PLOTS

The events occur in such a way as to enable the reader to predict future events.

Ahlberg, Janet, and Allan Ahlberg. *Each Peach Pear Plum*. Harmondsworth: Kestrel, 1978.

Ahlberg, Janet, and Allan Ahlberg. *Peepo!* London: Viking, 1981.

Barton, Byron. *Buzz, Buzz, Buzz*. New York: Scholastic Press, 1973.

Burningham, John. *Mr. Grumpy's Outing*. New York: Scholastic Press, 1970.

Charlip, Remy. *Fortunately*. New York: Parents Magazine Press, 1971.

Charlip, Remy. *What Good Luck, What Bad Luck*. New York: Scholastic Press, 1964.

De Regniers, Beatrice Schenk. *Willy O'Dwyer Jumped in the Fire*. New York: Atheneum, 1968.

Higgins, Don. *Papa's Going to Buy Me a Mockingbird*. New York: Seabury Press, 1968.

Hutchins, Pat. *Titch*. New York: Macmillan, 1971.

Klein, Leonore. *Brave Daniel*. New York: Scholastic Press, 1958.

Nodset, Joan. *Who Took the Farmer's Hat?* New York: Scholastic Press, 1963.

Roffey, Maureen. *The Grand Old Duke of York*. London: Bodley Head, 1975.

Roffey, Maureen. *Tinker, Tailor, Soldier, Sailor*. London: Bodley Head, 1976.

Schulevitz, Uri. *One Monday Morning*. New York: Scribner, 1967.

Sendak, Maurice. *Where the Wild Things Are*. New York: Scholastic Press, 1973.

APPENDIX

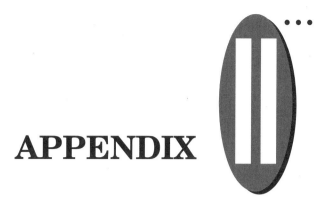

Generic questions for writing about books

SCHOOL STORIES

Do you ever feel like any of the children in this story?

In what ways is your school life like that in the book?

What do you notice about the groups of friends in your school and in the school in the book?

What different sorts of things do children learn in school and out of school?

Which children in the book enjoy school the most? Why do you think this is so?

How believable is school life in the story, e.g. are the teachers really like that?

Was there a conflict in this story? If so, between whom and why?

THE ODD ONE OUT

How would you feel if you were disabled in some way and were the odd one out?

What would you do if you were in the same situation as the main character?

How did the main character feel at the end of the story?

Why do you think the author wrote this story?

Could you suggest another ending?

In what ways did this person appear and behave differently from most children?

How do the other children and adults treat or react to the handicapped child? Why?

What do you think the handicapped child feels about his/her handicap?

How does the handicapped child cope with his or her handicap?

Do you feel sorry for the odd one out in this story? Why or why not? Should we feel sorry for people like him/her?

How do you think the author wants us to feel about the main character?

What do you think of the way the story ended, that is the resolution?

Would you like to change it?

COMEDY

Which moment in the story was the funniest?

Did you ever feel sorry for, or angry with, any of the characters? If so, when and why?

Was there a person, or incident, in the story that reminded you of a person, or incident, in another story/poem, play/television program you've seen or read?

Tell me the funniest joke you've ever heard.

Write a brief diary of events for the main character. Is the diary "funny"? If not, why not?

Is there someone you know who would enjoy this book? What would you tell him or her about the story to persuade him or her to read it?

Is there anything about the story that you would like to change? Why?

FAMILY STORY

Who are the main characters in the story?

What problems do these characters face and how do they solve them?

What is your favorite moment in the story?

How and why is the life of this family similar to or different from your own family's life?

If you had the choice, which character would you like to live with your family? Give your reasons.

Is there anyone in this family who is a bit like you? Why?

ADVENTURE STORIES

Is there a crime or wrongdoing that starts the actions of the book? Who does it?

Is there one main character in the story?

Why is this person the main character?

What sort of problems occur and how do the characters solve them?

Where and when does the adventure happen?

Are there any animals in the story? Are they important in the adventure? How?

Do adults have an important part? What role do adults play?

Does anyone get punished or caught for something he or she has done wrong? How does this happen?

Does the adventure turn out well in the end?

Did the adventure end the way you expected?

Would you like to have an adventure like the one in the story?

SCIENCE FICTION

Where and when does the story take place—in the past, present, or future?

Is time travel involved? Please explain.

How does the world of the story differ from the world as we know it?

Are there any characters in the story who are not human beings? Who are they? How are they different from human beings?

Do any of the characters possess extraordinary powers, e.g. ESP?

Would you like to live in the world of this story? If you could be anyone in this story, who would you choose and why?

Did you like the way the story ended? If not, how would you change it?

Can any of the robots in the story harm human beings?

How did you know this story is science fiction?

ANIMAL STORIES

Who are the animals in this story?

What sort of characteristics did they take on?

Do they seem more like people than real animals?

Are there any human beings in this story? How do they get on with the animals?

Do any of the animals remind you of people you know?

What happens to the animals in this story?

Do any of the animals change during the story?

What would the world be like if animals could talk?

How do your pets talk to you?

POETRY

Is the way that the poem is set out important? Would it still be a poem if it was set out as prose?

What do you like about the poem?

How was the author feeling when writing this poem?

What is your favorite poem?

How does this poem make you feel?

When the poem is read out loud, can you hear a rhythm?

Could you make this poem into a song or a piece of music?

What instruments would you use to express the feeling of the poem?

Are there any poems you know by heart? How did you come to know them by heart?

MYTHS AND LEGENDS

Is the story set in a real place or an imaginary one?

Who is the hero/heroine or main character of the story?

What extraordinary powers does the main character possess?

Was the main character of humble or divine birth? How does that affect his/her place in the story?

What was the main character's mission or task? Why was this important?

What did he/she have to give up in order to pursue the task?

What happened finally, as a result of the main characters' actions?

Why do you think this story was told in the first place?

What obstacles did the main character overcome?

MYSTERY STORIES

What was the actual mystery or crime in the novel?

Could you identify with any of the characters?

Was there a motive for the mystery or crime? If so what was it and which characters stood to benefit?

Was the setting in the novel crucial to the mystery? If so why?

What clues did the author give you to help you solve the mystery?

Did the author do anything to throw you off the track?

How was the mystery solved and by whom?

Were you satisfied with the ending? Please explain your answer.

Do you think the events in the book were realistic? Could such things really happen?

Do you think you could plan your own mystery story similar to the one in the book?

Did you solve the mystery before it was solved in the story?

How did you do it?

Were there questions still unanswered at the end?

How did the author build up the suspense?

FANTASY

Is the world in which the story is set similar to our world?

What are the differences?

What special traits or powers do the characters have that we do not?

Do the characters possess these powers at the beginning of the story? If not, how do they discover them?

Are there two opposing forces in the story? If so, what are they?

What are the problems faced by the main characters?

How do they solve these problems?

How has the author made the story believable?

If you had been part of the story how might you have used your one special power to resolve the conflict?

Did you enjoy this fantasy?

APPENDIX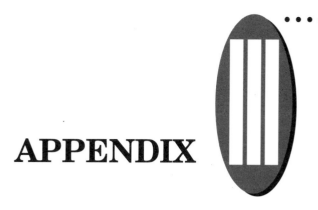

Children's book-award winners

CANADIAN BOOK-AWARD WINNERS

Canadian Library Association Book of the Year Award for Children

Presented annually to the author of the best children's book published in Canada for that year.

1947   *Starbuck Winter Valley* by Roderick Haig-Brown (William Morrow)

1948   No Award

1949   *Kristli's Trees* by Mabel Dunham (McClelland and Stewart)

1950   *Franklin of the Arctic* by Richard S. Lambert (McClelland and Stewart)

1951   No Award

1952   *The Sun Horse* by Catherine Anthony Clark (Macmillan)

1953   No Award

1954   No Award

1955   No Award

1956   *Train for Tiger Lily* by Louise Riley (Macmillan)

1957   *Glooscap's Country* by Cyrus Macmillan (Oxford)

1958   *Lost in the Barrens* by Farley Mowat (Little, Brown)

1959   *The Dangerous Cove* by John F. Hayes (Copp Clark)

1960   *The Golden Phoenix and Other French Canadian Fairy Tales* by Marius Barbeau and Michael Hornyansky (Oxford)

1961   *The St. Lawrence* by William Toye (Oxford)

1962   No Award

1963   *The Incredible Journey* by Sheila Burnford (Little, Brown Totem Books)

1964   *The Whale People* by Roderick Haig-Brown (Collins)

1965   *Tales of Nanabozho* by Dorothy M. Reid (Oxford)

1966   *Tikta'liktak* by James Houston (Longman)

   The Double Knights by James McNeill (Oxford)

1967   *Raven's Cry* by Christie Harris (McClelland and Stewart)

1968   *The White Archer* by James Houston (Academic Press)

1969   *And Tomorrow The Stars* by Kay Hill (Dodd Mead)

1970   *Sally Go Round the Sun* by Edith Fowke (McClelland and Stewart)

1971   *Cartier Discovers the St. Lawrence* by William Toye (Oxford)

1972   *Mary of Mile 18* by Ann Blades (Tundra Books)

1973   *The Marrow of the World* by Ruth Nichols (Macmillan)

1974   *The Miraculous Hind* by Elizabeth Cleaver (Holt, Rinehart and Winston)

1975   *Alligator Pie* by Dennis Lee (Macmillan)

1976   *Jacob Two-Two Meets the Hooded Fang* by Mordecai Richler (McClelland and Stewart)

1977   *Mouse Woman and the Vanished Princesses* by Christie Harris (McClelland and Stewart)

1978   *Garbage Delight* by Dennis Lee (Macmillan)

1979   *Hold Fast* by Kevin Major (Clarke, Irwin)

1980   *River Runners* by James Houston (McClelland and Stewart)

1981   *The Violin Maker's Gift* by Donn Kushner (Macmillan)

1982   *The Root Cellar* by Janet Lunn (Lester & Orpen Dennys)

1983   *Up To Low* by Brian Doyle (Groundwood)

1984   *Sweetgrass* by Jan Hudson (Tree Frog Press)

1985   *Mama's Going To Buy You a Mockingbird* by Jean Little (Penguin Books)

1986   *Julie* by Cora Taylor (Western Producer Prairie Books)

1987   *Shadow in Hawthorn Bay* by Janet Lunn (Lester & Orpen Dennys)

1988   *A Handful of Time* by Kit Pearson (Viking)

1989   *Easy Avenue* by Brian Doyle (Groundwood)

1990   *The Sky is Falling* by Kit Pearson (Viking)

1991   *Redwork* by Michael Bedard (Lester & Orpen Dennys)

1992   *Eating Between the Lines* by Kevin Major (Doubleday)

1993   *Ticket to Curlew* by Celia Lottridge (Groundwood)

1994   *Some of the Kinder Planets* by Tim Wynne-Jones (Groundwood)

The Amelia Frances Howard-Gibson Illustrator's Award
Given by the Canadian Association of Children's Librarians, this annual award goes to the best illustrated Canadian book published for children.

1971   *The Wind Has Wings* by Elizabeth Cleaver (Oxford)

1972   *A Child in a Prison Camp* by Shizuye Takashima (Tundra Books)

1973 *Au Dela du Soleil / Beyond the Sun* by Jacques de Roussan (Tundra Books)

1974 *A Prairie Boy's Winter* by William Kurelek (Tundra Books)

1975 *The Sleighs of My Childhood / Les Traineaux de Mon Enfance* by Carlo Italiano (Tundra Books)

1976 *A Prairie Boy's Summer* by William Kurelek (Tundra Books)

1977 *Down By Jim Long's Stage* by Al Pittman, ill. by Pam Hall (Breakwater Books)

1978 *The Loon's Necklace* by William Toye, ill. by Elizabeth Cleaver (Oxford)

1979 *Salmon for Simon* by Betty Waterton, ill. by Ann Blades (Douglas & McIntyre)

1980 *The Twelve Dancing Princesses* by Janet Lunn, ill. by Laszlo Gal (Methuen)

1981 *The Trouble with Princesses* by Christie Harris, ill. by Douglas Tait (McClelland and Stewart)

1982 *Ytek and the Arctic Orchid* by Garnet Hewitt, ill. by Heather Woodall (Douglas & McIntyre)

1983 *Chester's Barn* by Lindee Climo (Tundra Books)

1984 *Zoom at Sea* by Tim Wynne-Jones, ill. by Ken Nutt (Groundwood Books)

1985 *Chin Chiang and the Dragon's Dance* by Ian Wallace (Groundwood Books)

1986 *Zoom Away* by Tim Wynne-Jones, ill. by Ken Nutt (Groundwood Books)

1987 *Moonbeam on a Cat's Ear* by Marie-Louise Gay (Stoddart)

1988 *Rainy Day Magic* by Marie-Louise Gay (Stoddart)

1989 *Amos's Sweater* by Janet Lunn, ill. by Kim LaFave (Groundwood Books)

1990 *Til All The Stars Have Fallen* edited by David Booth, ill. by Kady MacDonald Denton (Kids Can Press)

1991 *The Orphan Boy* by Tololwa Mollel, ill. by Paul Morin (Oxford)

1992 *Waiting for the Whales* by Sheryl McFarlane, ill. by Ron Lightburn (Orca Books)

1993 *The Dragon's Pearl* by Julie Lawson, ill. by Paul Morin (Oxford)

1994 *Last Leaf, First Snowflake to Fall* by Leo Yerxa (Douglas and McIntyre)

AMERICAN BOOK-AWARD WINNERS

John Newbery Medal

1922 *The Story of Mankind* by Hendrik Willem van Loon (Liveright)

1923 *The Voyages of Doctor Dolittle* by Hugh Lofting (Lippincott)

1924 *The Dark Frigate* by Charles Hawes (Atlantic-Little)

1925 *Tales From Silver Lands* by Charles Finger (Doubleday)

1926 *Shen of the Sea* by Arthur Bowie Chrisman (Dutton)

1927 *Smoky, The Cowhorse* by Will James (Scribner)

1928 *Gayneck, The Story of a Pigeon* by Dhan Gopal Mukerji (Dutton)

1929 *The Trumpeter of Krakow* by Eric P. Kelly (Macmillan)

1930 *Hitty, Her First Hundred Years* by Rachel Field (Macmillan)

1931 *The Cat Who Went To Heaven* by Elizabeth Coatsworth (Macmillan)

1932 *Waterless Mountain* by Laura Adams Armer (Longmans)

1933 *Young Fu of the Upper Yangtze* by Elizabeth Lewis (Winston)

1934 *Invincible Louisa* by Cornelia Meigs (Little)

1935 *Dobry* by Monica Shannon (Viking)

1936 *Caddie Woodlawn* by Carol R. Brink (Macmillan)

1937 *Roller Skates* by Ruth Sawyer (Viking)

1938 *The White Stag* by Kate Seredy (Viking)

1939 *Thimble Summer* by Elizabeth Enright (Rinehart)

1940 *Daniel Boone* by James Daugherty (Viking)

1941 *Call It Courage* by Armstrong Sperry (Macmillan)

1942 *The Matchlock Gun* by Walter D. Edmonds (Dodd)

1943 *Adam of the Road* by Elizabeth Janet Gray (Viking)

1944 *Johnny Tremain* by Esther Forbes (Houghton)

1945 *Rabbit Hill* by Robert Lawson (Viking)

1946 *Strawberry Girl* by Lois Lenski (Lippincott)

1947 *Miss Hickory* by Carolyn S. Bailey (Viking)

1948 *The Twenty-one Balloons* by William Pene du Bois (Viking)

1949 *King of the Wind* by Marguerite Henry (Rand)

1950 *The Door in the Wall* by Marguerite de Angeli (Doubleday)

1951 *Amos Fortune Free Man* by Elizabeth Yates (Aladdin)

1952 *Ginger Pye* by Eleanor Estes (Harcourt)

1953 *Secret of the Andes* by Ann Nolan Clark (Viking)

1954 *And Now Miguel* by Joseph Krumgold (Crowell)

1955 *The Wheel on the School* by Meindert Delong (Harper)

1956 *Carry On, Mr. Bowditch* by Jean Lee Latham (Houghton)

1957 *Miracles On Maple Hill* by Virginia Sorensen (Harcourt)

1958 *Rifles for Watie* by Harold Keith (Crowell)

1959 *The Witch of Blackbird Pond* by Elizabeth George Speare (Houghton)

1960 *Onion John* by Joseph Krumgold (Crowell)

1961 *Island of the Blue Dolphins* by Scott O'Dell (Houghton)

1962 *The Bronze Bow* by Elizabeth George Speare (Houghton)

1963 *A Wrinkle in Time* by Madeleine l'Engle (Farrar)

1964 *It's Like This, Cat* by Emily Cheney Neville (Harper)

1965 *Shadow of a Bull* by Maia Wojciechowska (Atheneum)

1966 *I, Juan de Pareja* by Elizabeth Borten de Trevino (Farrar)

1967 *Up a Road Slowly* by Irene Hunt (Follett)

1968 *From the Mixed-up Files of Mrs. Basil E. Frankweiler* by E.L. Konigsburg (Atheneum)

1969 *The High King* by Lloyd Alexander (Holt)

1970 *Sounder* by William H. Armstrong (Harper)

1971 *Summer of the Swans* by Betsy Byars (Viking)

1972 *Mrs. Frisby and the Rats of Nimh* by Robert C. O'Brien (Atheneum)

1973 *Julie of the Wolves* by Jean Craighead George (Harper)

1974 *The Slave Dancer* by Paula Fox (Bradbury)

1975 *M.C. Higgins, The Great* by Virginia Hamilton (Macmillan)

1976 *The Grey King* by Susan Cooper (McElderry/Atheneum)

1977 *Roll of Thunder, Hear My Cry* by Mildred Taylor (Dial)

1978 *Bridge to Terabithia* by Katherine Paterson (Crowell)

1979 *The Westing Game* by Ellen Raskin (Dutton)

1980 *A Gathering of Days* by Joan M. Blos (Scribner)

1981 *Jacob Have I Loved* by Katherine Paterson (Crowell)

1982 *A Visit to William Blake's Inn: Poems For Innocent and Experienced Travellers* by Nancy Willard (Harcourt)

1983 *Dicey's Song* by Cynthia Voight (Atheneum)

1984 *Dear Mr. Henshaw* by Beverly Cleary (Morrow)

1985 *The Hero and the Crown* by Robin McKinley (MacRae)

1986 *Sarah, Plain and Tall* by Patricia McLachlan (HarperCollins)

1987 *Whipping Boy* by Sid Fleischman (Greenwillow)

1988 *Lincoln: A Photo Biography* by Russell Freedman (Clarion)

1989 *Joyful Noise* by Paul Fleischman (Harper & Row)

1990 *Number the Stars* by Lois Lowry (Houghton Mifflin)

1991 *Maniac Magee* by Jerry Spinelli (Little, Brown)

1992 *Shiloh* by Phyllis Reynolds Naylor (Atheneum)

1993 *Missing May* by Cynthia Rylant (Orchard Books)

1994 *The Giver* by Lois Lowry (Houghton Mifflin)

Randolph Caldecott Medal

Awarded annually since 1938, under the supervision of the Association for Library Services to Children of the American Library Association (50F Huron St., Chicago, IL 60611), to the illustrator of the most distinguished picture book for children published in the US during the preceding year.

1938 *Animals of the Bible* by Helen Dean Fish, ill. by Dorothy P. Lathrop (Lippincott)

1939 *Mei Li* by Thomas Handforth (Doubleday)

1940 *Abraham Lincoln* by Ingri & Edgar Parin d'Aulaire (Doubleday)

1941 *They Were Strong and Good* by Robert Lawson (Viking)

1942 *Make Way for Ducklings* by Robert McCloskey (Viking)

1943   *The Little House* by Virginia Lee Burton (Houghton)

1944   *Many Moons* by James Thurber, ill. by Louis Slobodkin (Harcourt)

1945   *Prayer For A Child* by Rachel Field, ill. by Elizabeth Orton Jones (Macmillan)

1946   *The Rooster Crows* (traditional Mother Goose), ill. by Maud & Miska Petersham (Macmillan)

1947   *The Little Island* by Golden MacDonald, ill. by Leonard Weisgard (Doubleday)

1948   *White Snow, Bright Snow* by Alvin Tresselt, ill. by Roger Duvoisin (Lothrop)

1949   *The Big Snow* by Berta & Elmer Hader (Macmillan)

1950   *Song of The Swallows* by Leo Politi (Scribner)

1951   *The Egg Tree* by Katherine Milhous (Scribner)

1952   *Finders Keepers* by Will, ill. by Nicholas (Harcourt)

1953   *The Biggest Bear* by Lynd Ward (Houghton)

1954   *Madeline's Rescue* by Ludwig Bemelmans (Viking)

1955   *Cinderella or the Little Glass Slipper* by Charles Perrault, trans. & ill. by Marcia Brown (Scribner)

1956   *Frog Went A-Courtin'* ed. by John Langstaff, ill. by Feodor Rojankovsky (Harcourt)

1957   *A Tree is Nice* by Janice May Udry, ill. by Marc Simont (Harper)

1958   *Time of Wonder* by Robert McCloskey (Viking)

1959   *Chanticleer and The Fox* adapted from Chaucer & ill. by Barbara Cooney (Crowell)

1960   *Nine Days to Christmas* by Marie Hall Ets & Aurora Labastida, ill. by Marie Hall Ets (Viking)

1961   *Baboushka and the Three Kings* by Ruth Robbins, ill. by Nicholas Sidjakev (Parnassus)

1962   *Once a Mouse* by Marcia Brown (Scribner)

1963   *The Snowy Day* by Ezra Jack Keats (Viking)

1964   *Where the Wild Things Are* by Maurice Sendak (Harper)

1965   *May I Bring A Friend?* by Beatrice Schenk de Regniers, ill. by Beni Montresor (Atheneum)

1966   *Always Room For One More* by Sorche Nic Leodhas, ill. by Nonny Hogrogian (Holt)

1967   *Sam, Bangs and Moonshine* by Evaline Ness (Holt)

1968   *Drummer Hoff* by Barbara Emberley, ill. by Ed Emberley (Prentice)

1969   *The Fool of the World and the Flying Ship* by Arthur Ransome, ill. by Uri Shulevitz (Farrar)

1970   *Sylvester and the Magic Pebble* by William Steig (Windmill/Simon & Schuster)

1971   *A Story – A Story* by Gail E. Haley (Atheneum)

1972   *One Fine Day* by Nonny Hogrogian (Macmillan)

1973   *The Funny Little Woman* retold by Arlene Mosel, ill. by Blair Lent (Dutton)

1974   *Duffy and the Devil* by Harve Zemach, ill. by Margot Zemach (Farrar)

1975   *Arrow to the Sun* by Gerald McDermott (Viking)

1976   *Why Mosquitoes Buzz in People's Ears* by Verna Aardema, ill. by Leo & Diane Dillon (Dial)

1977　*Ashanti to Zulu: African Traditions* by Margaret Musgrove, ill. by Leo & Diane Dillon (Dial)

1978　*Noah's Ark* by Peter Spier (Doubleday)

1979　*The Girl Who Loved Wild Horses* by Paul Goble (Bradbury)

1980　*The Ox Cart Man* by Donald Hall, ill. by Barbara Cooney (Viking)

1981　*Fables* by Arnold Lobel (Harper & Row)

1982　*Jumanji* by Chris van Allsburg (Houghton)

1983　*Shadow* by Marcia Brown (Scribner)

1984　*The Glorious Flight* by Alice & Martin Provensen (Viking)

1985　*St. George and the Dragon* retold by M. Hodges, ill. by Trina Schart Hyman (Little, Brown)

1986　*Polar Express* by Chris van Allsburg (Houghton)

1987　*Hey, Al* by Arthur Yorinks (Farrar)

1988　*Owl Moon* by Jane Yolen, ill. by John Schoenherr (Philomel Books)

1989　*Song and Dance Man* by Karen Ackerman, ill. by Stephen Gammell (Knopf)

1990　*Lon Po Po* by Ed Young (Philomel Books)

1991　*Black and White* by David MacAuley (Houghton Mifflin)

1992　*Tuesday* by David Weisner (Clarion Books)

1993　*Mirette on the High Wire* by Emily McCully (Putnam)

1994　*Grandfather's Journey* by Allan Say (Houghton Mifflin)

AUSTRALIAN BOOK-AWARD WINNERS

Children's Books of the Year

1946　*Karrawingi, the Emu* by Leslie Rees (Sands)

1947　No Award

1948　*Shackleton's Argonauts* by Frank Hurley (Angus & Robertson)

1949　*Whalers of the Midnight Sun* by Alan Villiers (Angus & Robertson)

1950　No Award

1951　*Verity of Sydney Town* by Ruth Williams (Angus & Robertson)

1952　*The Australia Book* by Eve Pownall (Sands)

1953　*Aircraft of Today & Tomorrow* by J.H. & W.D. Martin (Angus & Robertson)

　　　Good Luck to the Rider by Joan Phipson (Angus & Robertson)

1954　*Australian Legendary Tales* by K.L. Parker (Angus & Robertson)

1955　*The First Walkabout* by H.A. Lindsay & N.B. Tindale (Kestrel)

1956　*Wish and the Magic Nut* by Peggy Barnard, ill. by Sheila Hawkins (Sands) P

　　　The Crooked Snake by Patricia Wrightson (Angus & Robertson) B/Y

1957　No Picture Book Award

　　　The Boomerang Book of Legendary Tales by Enid Moodie-Heddle (Kestrel) B/Y

1958   *Piccaninny Walkabout* by Axel Poignant (Angus & Robertson) P

       Tiger in the Bush by Nan Chauncy (Oxford) B/Y

1959–
1964   No Picture Book Awards

1959   *Devil's Hill* by Nan Chauncy (Oxford) B/Y

       Sea Menace by John Gunn (Constable) B/Y

1960   *All the Proud Tribesmen* by Kylie Tennant (Macmillan) B/Y

1961   *Tangara* by Nan Chauncy (Oxford) B/Y

1962   *The Racketty Street Gang* by H.L. Evers (Hodder & Stoughton) B/Y

       Rafferty Rides a Winner by Joan Woodbery (Parrish) B/Y

1963   *The Family Conspiracy* by Joan Phipson (Angus & Robertson) B/Y

1964   *The Green Laurel* by Eleanor Spence (Oxford) B/Y

1965   *Hugo's Zoo* by Elisabeth MacIntyre (Angus & Robertson) P

       Pastures of the Blue Crane by Hesba F. Brinsmead (Oxford) B/Y

1966–
1968   No Picture Book Awards

1966   *Ash Road* by Ivan Southall (Angus & Robertson) B/Y

1967   *The Min Min* by Mavis Thorpe Clark (Landsdowne) B/Y

1968   *To the Wild Sky* by Ivan Southall (Angus & Robertson) B/Y

1969   *Sly Old Wardrobe* by Ivan Southall, ill. by Ted Greenwood (Cheshire) P

       When Jays Fly to Barbmo by Margaret Balderson (Oxford) B/Y

1970   No Picture Book Award

       Uhu by Annette Macarther-Onslow (Ure Smith) B/Y

1971   *Waltzing Matilda* by A.B. Paterson, ill. by Desmond Digby (Collins Australia) P

       Bread and Honey by Ivan Southall (Angus & Robertson) B/Y

1972   No Picture Book Award

       Longtime Passing by Hesba F. Brinsmead (Angus & Robertson) B/Y

1973   No Picture Book Award

       Family at the Lookout by Noreen Shelly (Oxford) B/Y

1974   *The Bunyip of Berkeley's Creek* by Jenny Wagner, ill. by Ron Brooks (Kestrel) P

       The Nargun and the Stars by Patricia Wrightson (Hutchinson) B/Y

       Mulga Bill's Bicycle by A.B. Paterson, ill. by Kilmeny & Deborah Niland (Collins Australia) V/A

1975   *The Man from Ironbark* by A.B. Paterson, ill. by Quentin Hole (Collins Australia) P

       No Book of the Year Award

       Storm Boy by Colin Thiele, ill. by Robert Ingpen (Rigby) V/A

       The Magpie Island by Colin Thiele, ill. by Roger Haldane (Rigby) V/A

1976   *The Rainbow Serpent* by Dick Roughsey (Collins Australia) P

       Fly West by Ivan Southall (Angus & Robertson) B/Y

Terry's Brrrmmm GT by Ted Greenwood (Angus & Robertson) V/A

1977 *ABC of Monsters* by Deborah Niland (Hodder & Stoughton Australia) P

The October Child by Eleanor Spence (Oxford) B/Y

1978 *John Brown, Rose and the Midnight Cat* by Jenny Wagner, ill. by Ron Brooks (Kestrel) P

The Ice Is Coming by Patricia Wrightson (Hutchinson Australia) B/Y

1979 *The Quinkins* written & ill. by Percy Trezise & Dick Roughsey (Collins Australia) P

The Plum-Rain Scroll by Ruth Manley (Hodder & Stoughton Australia) B/Y

1980 *Displaced Person* by Lee Harding (Hyland House) B/Y

1981 *Playing Beatie Bow* by Ruth Park (Nelson) B/Y

No Picture Book Award

1982 *The Valley Between* by Colin Thiele (Rigby) B/Y

Sunshine by Jan Ormerod (Kestrel) P

1983 *Master of the Grove* by Victor Kelleher (Kestrel) B/Y

Who Sank the Boat by Pamela Allen (Hamish Hamilton) P

Junior Book of the Year – *Thing* by Robin Klein (OUP)

1984 *A Little Fear* by Patricia Wrightson (Hutchinson) B/Y

Bertie and the Bear by Pamela Allen (Nelson) P

Junior Book of the Year – *Bernice Knows Best* by Max Dann (OUP)

1985 *The True Story of Lilli Stubeck* by James Aldridge (Hyland House)

No Picture Book Award

1986 *The Green Wind* by Thurley Fowler (Rigby) B/Y

Arkwright by Mary Steele (Hyland House) Y

Felix & Alexander by Terry Denton (Oxford) P

1987 *All We Know* by Simon French (Angus & Robertson) B/Y

Pigs Might Fly by Emily Rodda (Angus & Robertson) Y

Kojuro and the Bears adapted by Helen Smith; illustrated by Junko Morimoto (Collins) P

1988 *So Much to Tell You* by John Marsden (Walter McVitty) B/Y

My Place by Nadia Wheatley; ill. by Donna Rawlins (Collins Dove) Y

Crusher Is Coming by Bob Graham (Lothian) P

1989 *Beyond the Labyrinth* by Gillian Rubinstein (Hyland House) B/Y

The Best-Kept Secret by Emily Rodda (Angus & Robertson) Y

Drac and the Gremlin by Allan Baillie; ill. by Jane Tanner (Viking Kestrel) P

The Eleventh Hour by Graeme Base (Viking Kestrel) P

1990 *Came Back to Show You I Could Fly* by Robin Klein (Viking Kestrel) B/Y

Pigs and Honey by Jeannie Adams (Omnibus) Y

The Very Best of Friends by Margaret Wild; ill. by Julie Vivas (Margaret Hamilton) P

1991 *Strange Objects* by Gary Crew (Heinemann) B/Y

Finders Keepers by Emily Rodda (Omnibus) Y

Greetings from Sandy Beach by Bob Graham (Lothian) P

1992 *The House Guest* by Eleanor Nilsson (Viking) B/Y

The Magnificent Nose and Other Marvels by Anna Sienberg; ill. by Kim Gamble (Allen & Unwin) Y

Window by Jeanie Baker (Julia MacRae) P

1993 *Looking for Alibrandi* by Melina Marchetta (Penguin) B/Y

The Bamboo Flute by Gary Disher (Collins Angus & Robertson) Y

Rose Meets Mr Wintergarten by Bob Graham (Viking) P

BRITISH BOOK-AWARD WINNERS

Carnegie Medal

Given annually since 1937 by the British Library Association for a children's book of outstanding merit written in English and first published in the United Kingdom during the preceding year.

1936 *Pigeon Post* by Arthur Ransome (Cape)

1937 *The Family from One End Street* by Eve Garnett (Muller)

1938 *The Circus Is Coming* by Noel Streatfield (Dent)

1939 *Radium Woman* by Eleanor Doorly (Heinemann)

1940 *Visitors from London* by Kitty Barne (Dent)

1941 *We Couldn't Leave Dinah* by Mary Treadgold (Penguin)

1942 *The Little Grey Men* by BB (Eyre & Spottiswoode)

1943 No Award

1944 *The Wind on the Moon* by Eric Linklater (Macmillan)

1945 No Award

1946 *The Little White Horse* by Elizabeth Goudge (Brockhampton Press)

1947 *Collected Stories for Children* by Walter de la Mare (Faber)

1948 *Sea Change* by Richard Armstrong (Dent)

1949 *The Story of Your Home* by Agnes Allen (Transatlantic)

1950 *The Lark on the Wing* by Elfrida Vipont Foulds (Oxford)

1951 *The Wool-Pack* by Cynthia Harnett (Methuen)

1952 *The Borrowers* by Mary Norton (Dent)

1953 *A Valley Grows Up* by Edward Osmond (Oxford)

1954 *Knight Crusader* by Ronald Welch (Oxford)

1955 *The Little Bookroom* by Eleanor Farjeon (Oxford)

1956 *The Last Battle* by C.S. Lewis (Bodley Head)

1957 *A Grass Rope* by William Mayne (Oxford)

1958 *Tom's Midnight Garden* by Philippa Pearce (Oxford)

1959 *The Lantern Bearers* by Rosemary Sutcliff (Oxford)

1960 *The Making of Man* by I.W. Cornwall (Phoenix House)

1961 *A Stranger at Green Knowe* by Lucy Boston (Faber)

1962 *The Twelve and the Genii* by Pauline Clarke (Faber)

1963 *Time of Trial* by Hester Burton (Oxford)

1964 *Nordy Bank* by Sheena Porter (Oxford)

1965 *The Grange at High Force* by Philip Turner (Oxford)

1966 No Award

1967 *The Owl Service* by Alan Garner (Collins)

1968 *The Moon in the Cloud* by Rosemary Harris (Faber)

1969 *The Edge of the Cloud* by K.M. Peyton (Oxford)

1970 *The God Beneath the Sea* by Leon Garfield & Edward Blishen (Kestrel)

1971 *Josh* by Ivan Southall (Angus & Robertson)

1972 *Watership Down* by Richard Adams (Rex Collings)

1973 *The Ghost of Thomas Kempe* by Penelope Lively (Heinemann)

1974 *The Stronghold* by Mollie Hunter (Hamilton)

1975 *The Machine Gunner* by Robert Westall (Macmillan)

1976 *Thunder and Lightnings* by Jan Mark (Kestrel)

1977 *The Turbulent Term of Tyke Tiler* by Gene Kemp (Faber)

1978 *Exeter Blitz* by David Rees (Heinemann)

1979 *Tulka* by Peter Dickinson (Gollancz)

1980 *City of Gold* by Peter Dickinson (Gollancz)

1981 *The Scarecrows* by Robert Westall (Chatto & Windus)

1982 *The Haunting* by Margaret Mahy (Dent)

1983 *Handles* by Jan Mark (Kestrel)

1984 *The Changeover* by Margaret Mahy (Dent)

1985 *Storm* by Kevin Crossley-Holland (Heinemann)

1986 *Granny Was a Buffer Girl* by Berlie Doherty (Methuen)

1987 *Ghost Drum* by Susan Price (Faber)

1988 *Pack of Lies* by Geraldine McCaughrean (Oxford)

1989 *Goggle Eyes* by Anne Fine (H. Hamilton)

1990 *Wolf* by Gillian Cross (Oxford)

1991 *Dear Nobody* by Berlie Doherty (H. Hamilton)

1992 *Flour Babies* by Anne Fine (H. Hamilton)

1993 *Stone Cold* by Robert Swindle

Kate Greenaway Medal
Given annually by the British Library Association (7 Ridgemount St., Store St, London W.C.1. England) to the most distinguished work in the illustration of children's books first published in the United Kingdom during the preceding year.

1956 *Tim All Alone* by Edward Ardizzone (Oxford)

1957 *Mrs. Easter and the Storks* by V.H. Drummond (Faber)

1958 No Award

1959 *Kashtanka and a Bundle of Ballads* by William Stobbs (Oxford)

1960 *Old Winkle and the Seagulls* by Elizabeth Rose, ill. by Gerald Rose (Faber)

1961 *Mrs Cockle's Cat* by Philippa Pearce, ill. by Anthony Maitland (Kestrel)

1962 *Brian Wildsmith's A B C* by Brian Wildsmith (Oxford)

1963 *Borka* by John Burningham (Cape)

1964 *Shakespeare's Theatre* by C.W. Hodges (Oxford)

1965 *Three Poor Tailors* by Victor Ambrus (Hamilton)

1966 *Mother Goose Treasury* by Raymond Briggs (Hamilton)

1967 *Charlie, Charlotte and the Golden Canary* by Charles Keeping (Oxford)

1968 *Dictionary of Chivalry* by Grant Uden, ill. by Pauline Baynes (Kestrel)

1969 *The Quangle-Wangle's Hat* by Edward Lear, ill. by Helen Oxenbury (Heinemann)

Dragon of an Ordinary Family by Margaret Mahy, ill. by Helen Oxenbury (Heinemann)

1970 *Mr Gumpy's Outing* by John Burningham (Cape)

1971 *The Kingdom Under the Sea* by Jan Pienkowski (Cape)

1972 *The Woodcutter's Duck* by Krystyna Turska (Hamilton)

1973 *Father Christmas* by Raymond Briggs (Hamilton)

1974 *The Wind Blew* by Pat Hutchins (Bodley Head)

1975 *Horses in Battle* by Victor Ambrus (Oxford)

Mishka by Victor Ambrus (Oxford)

1976 *The Post Office Cat* by Gail E. Haley (Bodley Head)

1977 *Dogger* by Shirley Hughes (Bodley Head)

1978 *Each Peach Pear Plum* by Alan Ahlberg, ill. by Janet Ahlberg (Kestrel)

1979 *Haunted House* by Jan Pienkowski (Heinemann)

1980 *Mister Magnolia* by Quentin Blake (Cape)

1981 *The Highwayman* by A. Noyes, ill. by Charles Keeping (Oxford)

1982 *Long Neck & Thunderfoot* by H. Piers, ill. by Michael Foreman (Kestrel)

Sleeping Beauty and Other Favourite Tales by A. Carter, ill. by Michael Foreman (Gollancz)

1983 *Gorilla* by Anthony Browne (MacRae)

1984 *Hiawatha's Childhood* by Errol Le Cain (Faber)

1985 *Sir Gawain and the Lothly Lady* by Selina Hastings, ill. by Juan Wijngaard (Walker)

1986 *Snow White in New York* by Fiona French (Oxford)

1987 *Crafty Chameleon* by Mwenye Hadithi, ill. by Adrienne Kennaway (Hodder and Stoughton)

1988 *Can't You Sleep, Little Bear?* by Martin Waddell, ill. by Barbara Firth (Candlewick Press)

1989 *War Boy* by Michael Foreman (Pavilion/M. Joseph)

1990 *Whales' Song* by Dyan Sheldon, ill. by Gary Blythe (Hutchinson)

1991 *The Jolly Christmas Postman* by Janet and Alan Ahlberg (Little, Brown)

1992 *Zoo* by Anthony Browne (McRae)

1993 *Black Ships Before Troy* by Rosemary Sutcliffe, ill. by Allan Lee

REFERENCES

Alderman, Belle, and Laureen Harman (eds.). *The Imagineers: Writing and Illustrating Children's Books*. Sydney: Wentworth Press, 1983.

Applebee, A. *The Child's Concept of Story: Ages Two to Seventeen*. Chicago: University of Chicago Press, 1978.

Atwell, N. "Writing and Reading Literature from the Inside Out." *Language Arts* 61, 3, 1984.

Bettelheim, B. *The Uses of Enchantment: The Meaning and Importance of Fairytales*. New York: Vintage, 1977.

Bloom, B. *Stability and Change in Human Characteristics*. New York: Wiley, 1964.

———. *Taxonomy of Educational Objectives. Handbook 1: Cognitive Domain*. New York: David McKay, 1956.

Burke, E.M. "Using Trade Books to Intrigue Children with Words." *The Reading Teacher* 32, 2, 1979.

Chomsky, C. "Stages in Language Development and Reading Exposure." *Harvard Educational Review* 42, February 1973.

Chukovsky, Kornei. *From Two to Five*. Berkeley: University of California Press, 1963.

Comber, B. "Classroom Explorations in Critical Literacy." *Australian Journal of Reading*, Vol. 16, No. 1, pp. 73-83, 1993.

Coody, B., and Nelson, D. *Teaching Elementary Language Arts: A Literature Approach*. Belmont, CA: Wadsworth, 1982.

Dansereau, D. "Co-operative Learning in Dyads." *Journal of Reading*, Vol. 29, No. 6, pp. 516-520, 1986.

Eagleton, T. *Literacy Theory: An Introduction*. Oxford: Basil Blackwell, 1983.

Edwards, P. *Hey That's A Good Idea: Useful Hints for Busy Teachers*. Primary English Teachers Association, 1985.

Fox, Mem. *Thereby Hangs a Tale*. Adelaide: Sturt CAE, 1980.

Frye, N. *The Educated Imagination*. Bloomington, IN: University of Indiana Press, 1964.

Galda, L. "Research in Response to Literature." *Journal of Research and Development in Education* 16, 3, 1983.

Hardy, B. *The Appropriate Form: An Essay on the Novel*. The Athlone Press, University of London, 1968.

Hickman, J. "Looking at Response to Literature" in Jaggar, Angela and Smith-Burke, M. Trika (eds.). *Observing the Language Learner*. New York: NCTE IRA, 1985.

Hill, S., and J. Hancock. *Reading and Writing Communities: Co-operative Literacy Learning in the Classroom*. Melbourne, Australia: Eleanor Curtain, 1993.

Hill, S., and Timothy H. Hill. *The Collaborative Classroom*. Melbourne, Australia: Eleanor Curtain, 1990.

Hill, S. "What Are Children Reading?" *Australian Journal of Reading* 7, 4, November 1984.

Holdaway, D. *The Foundation of Literacy*. Sydney: Ashton Scholastic, 1979.

Huck, C.S. *Children's Literature in the Elementary Schools*. 3rd ed. New York: Holt, Rinehart and Winston, 1976.

————. "Literature as the Content of Reading." *Theory Into Practice* 16, 4, December 1977.

Kagan, Spencer. *Co-operative Learning: Resources for Teachers*. Resources for Teachers: Capistrano, CA: San Juan, 1990.

Kemp, Max. "Monitoring Reading Progress" in Burnes, D. and Page, G. (eds.). *Insights and Strategies for Teaching Reading*. New York: Harcourt Brace Jovanovich, 1985.

Kirkpatrick, D.L. *Twentieth Century Children's Writers*, 2nd ed. London: Macmillan, 1983.

Koeller, Shirley. "25 Years Advocating Children's Literature in the Reading Program." *The Reading Teacher* 34, 5, February 1981.

Leavis, F.R. *English Literature in Our Time and the University*. London: Chatto and Windus, 1969.

Lukens, Rebecca. "The Child, the Critic and a Good Book." *Language Arts* 55, 4, April 1978.

Meek, Margaret. *Learning to Read*. London: Bodley Head, 1982.

Mikkelsen, N. "Talking and Telling: The Child as Story Maker." *Language Arts* 61, 3, March 1984.

Miller, J. "To Preserve Human-ness: Language and Literature in the 70s and Beyond." *Language Arts* 56, 9, September 1979.

Norton, D. *Through the Eyes of a Child: An Introduction to Children's Literature*. Columbus: Merrill, 1983.

Noyce, Ruth M. "Team Up and Teach with Trade Books." *The Reading Teacher* 32, 4, January 1979.

O'Sullivan, C. "Fifteen Ways Around a Traditional Tale." *Reading Around Series* 3, Australian Reading Association, 1984.

Petrosky, A.R. "The Inferences We Make: Children and Literature." *Language Arts* 57, 2, Feb. 1980.

Rosenblatt, Louise M. *The Reader, the Text, the Poem: the Transactional Theory of the Literary Work*. Edwardsville, IL: Southern Illinois University Press, 1978.

Sapon-Shevin, Mara. *Co-operative Learning, Co-operative Visions Connections*. Vol. 2, No. 4, pp. 25-31, 1993.

Stewig, J. *Children and Literature*. Chicago: Rand McNally, 1980.

————. *Live Wire: Classroom Ideas K–7.* New York: NCTE, 1984.

Sloan, Glenna. *The Child as Critic: Teaching Literature in the Elementary School.* New York: Teachers College, Columbia University, 1975.

————. "Commentary." *The Reading Teacher* 34, 2, 1980.

Tonkiss, Mark. "Pamela Allen." *Review*, December 1984.

Vygotsky, L.S. *Thought and Language.* Edited and translated by E. Hanfmann and G. Vakar. Cambridge, MA: MIT Press, 1962.

INDEX

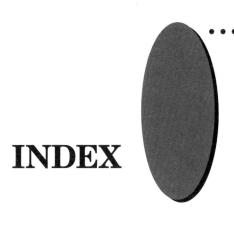